THE PLANT KITCHEN

THE PLANT KITCHEN

100 EASY RECIPES FOR VEGAN BEGINNERS

RYLAND PETERS & SMALL

LONDON • NEW YORK

Senior Designer Toni Kay
Editor Miriam Catley
Production David Hearn
Art Director Leslie Harrington
Editorial Director Julia Charles
Publisher Cindy Richards
Indexer Vanessa Bird

First published in 2020 by Ryland Peters & Small
20–21 Jockey's Fields, London WC1R 4BW
and
341 E 116th St, New York NY 10029
www.rylandpeters.com

10 9 8 7 6 5 4 3 2

ISBN: 978-1-78879-181-6

Printed in China

NOTES:
• Both British (Metric) and American (Imperial plus US
cups) measurements are included in these recipes for your
convenience, however it is important to work with one
set of measurements and not alternate between the
two within a recipe.
• All spoon measurements are level unless otherwise specified.
• All eggs are medium (UK) or large (US), unless specified
as large, in which case US extra-large should be used.
Uncooked or partially cooked eggs should not be served
to the very old, frail, young children, pregnant women
or those with compromised immune systems.
• Ovens should be preheated to the specified temperatures.
We recommend using an oven thermometer. If using a
fan-assisted oven, adjust temperatures according to the
manufacturer's instructions.
• When a recipe calls for the grated zest of citrus fruit, buy
unwaxed fruit and wash well before using. If you can only find
treated fruit, scrub well in warm soapy water before using.

CONTENTS

INTRODUCTION

Beginning to eat a plant-based diet might seem daunting at first. How will you get enough protein? How will you find the time to prepare complicated meat-free meals? And where will you source the special ingredients? The good news is that eating a vegan diet needn't mean lots of extra time and effort on your part. This collection of recipes aims to offer simple and nutritious recipes for dishes you'll want to make again and again. From lasagne to curry, pancakes to panna cotta, there is an easy plant-based recipe here that will satisfy your appetite and take you on voyage of vegan food discovery.

In the first section of the book you will learn how to make The Basics such as nut and seed milk and cheese and vegan mayonnaise. The next chapter offers a host of Breakfast & Brunch recipes that can be made ahead for the week or whipped up at the weekend for a leisurely brunch. Light Bites & Snacks includes a selection of moreish recipes such as hummus, crackers and butternut squash fries, that aim to help you resist the urge to buy convenience foods. Soups & Salads range from hearty and healthy to light and cleansing. Mid-Week Suppers offers the speediest recipes for satisfying dishes such as Thai Green Cauli Curry and an Azuki Bean Stew. In Feeding a Crowd you'll find many old favourites made vegan such as Spicy Sweet Potato Moussaka, a Mediterranean Green Lentil Loaf and Tex-Mex Tacos. And to round it all off there's a delicious selection of desserts and sweet things including cookies, cakes and ice-creams to satisfy the sweetest tooth.

THE BASICS

NUT & SEED MILK

Preparing your own nut or seed milk will save a fortune in the long run, and you'll be consuming a nutritionally superior drink in which all the enzymes remain intact.

150 g/1 cup nuts or seeds of your choosing
500 ml/2 cups water, for soaking
1 litre/4 cups water, for blending
3 dates or 2 tablespoons rice or agave syrup
    (optional)
1/4 teaspoon bourbon vanilla powder
    (optional)
cheese cloth or nut milk bag

Begin by soaking the nuts or seeds in water overnight. If you're in a hurry you can soak them for an hour or so, but overnight is best. Rinse and drain, discarding the soaking water.

Add the soaked nuts or seeds to your blender (high-speed blenders are most efficient for this), together with the water. Blend for a couple of minutes, until you have a smooth liquid without chunks. Now, use a double-folded cheese cloth or a nut-milk bag and strain the milk over a big bowl or jar. Squeeze really well to extract as much milk as possible. The residue on the cheese cloth or nut-milk bag is nut or seed flour, which you can add to smoothies, raw cakes or cracker dough (but make sure to use it within 2–3 days); alternatively you can dehydrate this flour on a very low temperature in the oven and you'll then be able to use it in bread, cakes and cookie mixes.

Raw nut and seed milk is very mild in flavour so, if you want to enhance the flavour to make it more appealing for children, for example, you can blend in the dates or rice or agave syrup and some vanilla. It's best to make the milk fresh and use it immediately, but it will keep in the fridge for up to two days.

ALMOND AND CASHEW NUT CHEESE

CHEESE STARTER (REJUVELAC)
40 g/1/4 cup sprouted spelt berries
    (a tiny white tail is enough)
470 ml/2 cups water

CHEESE
270 g/2 cups blanched almonds and/or
    cashew nuts, soaked overnight
110 ml/1/2 cup rejuvelac
1/4 teaspoon sea salt
2 garlic cloves, crushed
2 tablespoons olive oil
cheese cloth

Nut and seed cheeses are a great alternative to dairy and if you crave conventional cheese sometimes, this recipe might help you to overcome that!

Place the berries and water in a jar, cover with paper towel or a cheese cloth, and store in a warm place for 48 hours, or until the mixture turns fizzy and a little sour. In winter you'll need to either put the mixture close to the radiator, or leave it to ferment for at least a week at room temperature. Drain, keep the liquid and discard the berries. Instead of spelt berries, you can also use rye berries, unhulled millet, buckwheat, and even brown rice.

Drain the nuts and place them in a high-speed blender or food processor. Add the rejuvelac, garlic, salt and oil and blend until completely smooth. Line a sieve/strainer with two layers of cheese cloth, and spoon in the mixture before leaving it to set in a warm place for 24–48 hours. Then, form the mixture into the desired shape. Leave it covered with the cheese cloth. Leave in the refrigerator to finish setting for another day before serving. This is a soft cheese, and will keep in the fridge for about 10 days. Use it with crackers, bread, on top of vegetables or use it as a cheese substitute on pizza, before or after baking – it's up to you! Also, feel free to use herbs and spices in addition to or instead of the garlic; crushed black pepper, oregano, thyme, paprika, etc. all work well. Sunflower seeds mixed with cashews work well too, even though the colour isn't completely white.

MACADAMIA NUT CHEESE

This recipe can be used as a blueprint for your own cheese – play around with the flavourings, amount of water, and shape to create unlimited variations.

140 g/2 cups macadamia nuts
about 250 ml/1 cup warm water
2 probiotic supplement capsules
   (such as Acidophilus or a
   broad-spectrum probiotic)
½ teaspoon sea salt
1 tablespoon nutritional yeast
2 tablespoons black olives, chopped
1 tablespoon lemon juice
seed crackers, to serve
a high-speed blender
a colander lined with cheesecloth

Serves 2

Put the macadamia nuts in a high-speed blender with just enough warm water to cover them. Tip in the contents of the probiotic capsules and blend slowly until you have a completely smooth but thick mixture – if it easily forms peaks when a fork is dipped into the mixture, you know you're on the right track, but ensure the blender is switched off at the mains before testing.

Pour the mixture into the lined colander, fold the edges of the cloth over the top and press down gently to squeeze any excess moisture out of the nut mixture. Place a small plate on top of it and something heavy (a filled jar, can or book) on top of that. Leave the mixture to sit at room temperature for at least 24 hours to give it time to ferment and develop that 'cheesy' flavour.

Transfer the fermented nut mixture to a bowl and stir in the sea salt, nutritional yeast, chopped black olives and lemon juice.

Lay a sheet of parchment paper on a clean work surface and tip the nut mixture out onto it. Wrap the paper around the mixture and roll to shape into a log. Twist the ends to seal and chill in the fridge for about 6 hours before serving with seed crackers.

VEGAN PARMESAN

Traditional Parmesan is used in a multitude of dishes. This vegan version works well as a replacement to add that very unique umami, salt and even cheesy flavour.

150 g/1¼ cups unroasted cashews
¼ teaspoon garlic powder
4 tablespoons nutritional yeast
1 teaspoon salt

Makes 170 g/6 oz

Place all the ingredients in a small food processor and blitz until it becomes a coarse powder. Transfer to an airtight container and store in the cupboard for up to 1 week.

TOFU MAYONNAISE

We all know that the 'normal' mayonnaise is really unhealthy. Also, there are many vegan substitutes on the market that are almost equally unhealthy, with high levels of saturated fats and additives. Once you start making these healthy vegan mayonnaises, you won't look back.

300 g/10 oz. fresh tofu
6 tablespoons water
4 tablespoons olive or sunflower oil
3 tablespoons lemon juice or apple cider vinegar
1 soft date
½ teaspoon sea salt

Makes
350 g / 1½ cups

Blend all the ingredients in a blender until the mixture is completely smooth. Taste and adjust the seasonings. If you like it more tangy than sweet, add a little more lemon juice or vinegar. Also, pay attention to what you will serve it with. If you use it as a salad dressing, it needs to be a little bit more sour, so add a little more lemon juice or vinegar; if used with salty foods like burgers or chips, make it less salty.

SUNFLOWER & CASHEW MAYONNAISE

85 g/²/₃ cup sunflower seeds
95 g/²/₃ cup cashews
3 tablespoons olive oil
¾ teaspoon sea salt
4 tablespoons lemon juice
1 soft date
200 ml/¾ cup cold water
1 tablespoon apple cider vinegar
2 garlic cloves, peeled (optional)

Makes
400 ml / 1²/₃ cups

Soak the seeds and nuts in cold water overnight, then drain, discarding the liquid, rinse and drain again. Add them to the blender with all the other ingredients and blend until completely smooth. For the best results, use a high-speed blender to achieve a lovely velvety consistency.

For serving, follow the instructions for Tofu Mayonnaise above so that you don't make it too bland or too salty.

HUMMUS

320 g/2 cups chickpeas plus 60 ml/¼ cup of the liquid from the can, or more if needed, plus 2 tablespoons chickpeas to serve
2 tablespoons extra-virgin olive oil, plus 2 tablespoons to serve
1 tablespoon tahini
3 garlic cloves
freshly squeezed juice of ½ a lemon, or to taste
½ teaspoon salt, or to taste
freshly chopped flat-leaf parsley, to garnish (optional)

Makes about 2–4 servings

Hummus is often a staple food for those following a plant-based diet. Chickpeas are a good source of protein and fibre and are high in iron, folate, phosphorus and B vitamins.

Blend all the ingredients in a blender or food processor, except the extra chickpeas and olive oil to serve, slowly adding the cooking liquid until you reach a thick and creamy consistency; this will take about 1 minute. High-speed blenders make the creamiest texture and need less liquid and time, but both food processors and stick blenders can be used as well. Adjust the lemon juice and salt to taste.

Serve topped with 2 tablespoons extra-virgin olive oil and 2 tablespoons whole chickpeas. Garnish with chopped flat-leaf parsley, if you like.

VEGAN STUFFING

250 g/9 oz. tofu, seitan or tempeh
50 g/⅓ cup finely diced onion
4 tablespoons sunflower or olive oil
pinch of chilli powder
½ teaspoon ground ginger
¼ teaspoon ground turmeric
1 teaspoon dried herbes de Provence
3 teaspoons soy sauce
300 g/10½ oz. whole grains, cooked (brown rice, millet, quinoa, etc.)
2 tablespoons rolled oats or millet flakes
sea salt and crushed black pepper

It's fun to fill different types of vegetables, then bake or cook them for a quite impressive and really delicious result! The combination of protein, vegetables and grains makes this type of stuffing a complete meal. It's great used to stuff peppers, firm tomatoes, courgette/zucchini, as well as a filling for rice-paper rolls or spring rolls.

Mash the tofu or tempeh with a fork, or, if using seitan, put in a food processor with an S-blade to finely chop it. In a large frying pan/skillet over a low heat, sauté the onion until translucent, then add the dry spices and herbs and cook for a minute more. Add the soy sauce and bring up the heat. After the soy sauce is well incorporated, add the cooked grains and rolled oats or millet flakes and mix everything well before seasoning with salt and pepper to taste. When the stuffing looks like a thick risotto, it's ready for filling. Remember that the mixture will expand a little bit during cooking, so don't overfill the vegetables.

You can always make the stuffing a day or two in advance, as well as freeze it (if using tempeh or seitan, but not tofu) if you have leftovers.

4 tablespoons light sesame oil
pinch of sea salt
90 g/3 oz. onion
4 garlic cloves (optional)
1 tablespoon soy sauce
1 teaspoon apple cider vinegar
1 teaspoon rice or agave syrup
2 tablespoons unbleached plain/all-
    purpose flour
250 ml/1 cup water
2 teaspoons Dijon mustard
freshly ground black pepper
2 tablespoons chopped herbs, to garnish

Makes 500 ml/2 cups

ONION GRAVY

Slice the onions in thin half-moons lengthways. Add the sesame oil and salt to a large frying pan/skillet over a low heat and sauté the onions until they're translucent and soft. Add 4 crushed garlic cloves if desired, and cook until fragrant. Slightly bring up the heat, add the soy sauce, vinegar and syrup and stir well until it sizzles. Slowly add the flour and whisk vigorously for a minute, then, still whisking, add the water little-by-little until a gravy consistency is reached. Add mustard and pepper, taste and add more soy sauce if needed. Finally, sprinkle with chopped herbs to garnish, just before serving.

2 tablespoons crushed ginger
1/2 teaspoon ground ginger
2 tablespoons crushed garlic
3 tablespoons soy sauce
2 tablespoons toasted sesame oil
1 tablespoon rice or agave syrup
1/8 teaspoon chilli/chile powder
1 teaspoon freshly squeezed lemon juice
about 100 ml/1/3 cup water
2 tablespoons sesame seeds
3 tablespoons sliced spring onion/scallion

Makes 150 ml/2/3 cup

STIR-FRY SAUCE

Blend all the ingredients (except the sesame seeds and spring onion/scallion, which you'll add just before serving) in a food processor or blender until the mixture is fairly smooth.

50 g/ 2 oz. seaweed (such as laver,
    dulse or arame), cut into small strips
500 ml/2 cups light soy sauce or tamari
8 black peppercorns
2 garlic cloves, peeled
1 dried Chinese or shiitake mushroom

*Makes approx.
500 ml/2 cups*

VEGAN FISH SAUCE

Add 500 ml/2 cups of water to a medium pan and add the dried seaweed. Bring to the boil and then simmer for 30–40 minutes until the water has reduced by more than half. Let stand for an hour.

Strain the mixtures, reserving the liquid in another bowl. Rinse the pan and add the soy sauce or tamari, then add the peppercorns, garlic and dried mushrooms. Bring to a simmer, and add the seaweed reduction. Simmer for 30–40 minutes until the mixture has reduced to less than half again. Strain and store in a sterilized glass bottle in the fridge until needed.

SWEET NUT BUTTERS

PISTACHIO AND CACAO

230 g/2 cups pistachio nuts, shelled

200 ml/³/₄ cup almond milk

40 g/¹/₄ cup cacao nibs

1 teaspoon pure vanilla extract

a pinch of salt

a baking sheet, greased and lined with baking parchment

WALNUT AND COCONUT

150 g/1¹/₂ cups walnuts, soaked overnight and drained

40 g/¹/₂ cup desiccated/ shredded coconut

3 tablespoons coconut oil

160 ml/²/₃ cup almond milk

4 tablespoons coconut sugar

2 teaspoons pure vanilla extract

a pinch of salt

a baking sheet, greased and lined with baking parchment

NOT-TELLA

250 g/2 cups hazelnuts, peeled

200 ml/³/₄ cup almond milk

50 g/heaped ¹/₂ cup cacao powder

100 g/¹/₂ cup xylitol

1 teaspoon pure vanilla extract

a baking sheet, greased and lined with baking parchment

Each makes 600 ml (20 oz)/ 2¹/₂ cups

Here are a few new takes on plain nut and seed butters to try. They work well with coconut yogurt, served with pancakes or simply spread on toast.

Each of these spreads can be made in the same way. Preheat the oven to 180°C (350°F) Gas 4.

Spread the nuts on to the prepared baking sheet and bake in the preheated oven for about 10 minutes – you want them to be slightly browned but not burned.

Remove the sheet from the oven and allow the nuts to cool completely. Put them in a food processor with the remaining ingredients and pulse until you have a smooth and creamy nut butter.

These spreads are perfect for spreading on breads, celery sticks or even served as dips for vegetable sticks or crackers.

BREAKFAST & BRUNCH

ALKALIZING GREEN JUICE

5–6 Granny Smith or other apples
380 g/13 oz. or 1 small head organic
    cabbage
2 pomegranates
4 handfuls of green leafy vegetables
    (kale, chard, spinach, carrot greens,
    parsley, nettles, etc.)
½ lemon
15 g/½ oz. fresh ginger
about 360 ml/1½ cups water
1 teaspoon flaxseed, hemp or other oil

*Makes 1.4 litres/
1¼ quarts*

Make a commitment to your health goals and get a cold-press juicer.
It will change your life! Starting the day with a glass of freshly squeezed
veggie and fruit elixir will make you feel energized, nourished and light.

Wash all the fruit and vegetables. Slice the apples (leave the skin and pips)
and cabbage. Cut and break the pomegranates into segments. Next, divide
the seeds from their membranes. Peel the lemon and ginger and begin
juicing all the ingredients (except the water). Add a little of the water from
time to time (it's always a good idea to dilute pure juice with ¼ to ⅓ part
water to get an isotonic, rehydrating drink). Add the oil to the juice (this will
allow all the oil-soluble vitamins to be absorbed), stir and serve immediately.
If you have leftover juice, keep it refrigerated and drink it within 12 hours.

RAW COCOA MILKSHAKE

500 ml/2 cups Nut Milk (see page 10)
1 tablespoon raw cocoa powder
6 soft dates or 1 very ripe banana, peeled
¼ teaspoon bourbon vanilla powder
2 large handfuls of green leafy vegetables
    (dark kale, spinach, chard, etc.)

Serves 1–2

A combination of cocoa and greens, this milkshake will not only give
you energy but also a considerable amount of chlorophyll, which displays
antioxidant and anti-inflammatory properties, in addition to being a
good source of magnesium.

Add all the ingredients to the blender jug and blend until completely
smooth and foamy (a high-speed blender is the best option to achieve a
velvety consistency). Taste the mixture and adjust according to your liking:
to make it sweeter, add a couple more dates; add more cocoa powder for
an extra kick of flavour and energy. Depending on the season, adding fresh
strawberries, blueberries, apples or other sweet fruits will make the shake
taste slightly different (but still great) every day!

CARROT JUICE WITH BEETS & POMEGRANATE

6 carrots
2 beetroots/beets
2 pomegranates
250 ml/1 cup water
1 teaspoon flaxseed oil

Serves 1–2

Beetroot is full of iron but it is strong-tasting, so combining it with other fruits and veggies can help camouflage its earthy aroma. Carrots are a good juice base, and pomegranates serve here as a great C vitamin source, enabling the iron to be absorbed into the bloodstream.

Wash and slice the carrots and beetroots/beets, without peeling.

Cut and segment the pomegranates, dividing the seeds from the membranes. Start juicing, adding a little of the water from time to time. Add the oil to the juice, stir and serve immediately.

If you have leftover juice, keep it refrigerated and drink within 12 hours. If pomegranates are out of season, use oranges or lemons instead. Red cabbage works well instead of beetroot/beets, and will give this juice a fluorescent purple glow.

COCONUT & STRAWBERRY FRAPPÉ

250 ml/1 cup raw organic coconut water
500 ml/2 cups Nut Milk (see page 10)
400 g/4 cups strawberries
1 tablespoon nut butter
8 soft dates
few drops of freshly squeezed lemon juice

Serves 2

Coconut water is a great source of electrolytes necessary for proper hydration. Combined with freshly made nut milk, ripe strawberries and a couple of dates, this frappé will make you feel happy and hydrated!

Place all the ingredients into the blender jar, and mix until completely smooth and foamy. Drink immediately!

You can use any other fresh fruits you want, and add cocoa powder, spices and other dried fruits to make it sweeter. Raspberries, blackberries, apples or ripe apricots also make a great combination with the nut milk and coconut water.

STRAWBERRY, BANANA & ALMOND SMOOTHIE BOWL

200 g/2 cups strawberries, frozen
1 banana, peeled and frozen
60 g/generous ½ cup jumbo rolled oats
125 ml/½ cup almond milk
120 g/½ cup coconut yogurt
2 tablespoons almond butter
   (or any nut butter)
2 teaspoons pure maple syrup

TO SERVE
blueberries, sliced banana, toasted muesli,
   goji berries and/or chia seeds

Serves 1

This is definitely a dish for the Instagrammers as it looks so pretty with all of its colourful adornments. Feel free to substitute different fruits, nut butters and toppings that you have to hand. To make this a fast and easy weekday breakfast, freeze small bags with the banana, strawberries and oats ready to whizz up with the milk, yogurt and nut butter before adding your toppings.

Place all the smoothie ingredients into a blender and blitz until smooth.

Pour into a shallow bowl and decorate with blueberries, sliced banana, toasted muesli, goji berries and/or chia seeds. Serve.

AÇAI BOWLS GALORE

Having an açai bowl feels like eating ice cream for breakfast. If you are making these bowls for children, set up a toppings station and let them pick their own; it's a great way to start getting them more connected with what's going into their bodies.

1 pack frozen açai purée
   (about 100 ml/⅓ cup)
1 banana, peeled and frozen
200 ml/¾ cup almond milk

TO SERVE
20 g/¼ cup desiccated/shredded coconut
goji berries
strawberries, sliced banana or kiwi
   (optional)

Serves 2

Put the açai purée, frozen banana and almond milk in a food processor and blend together until smooth.

Pour the mixture into bowls and sprinkle with desiccated/shredded coconut and goji berries. Serve with fruit – a variety will work well here; try strawberries, banana or kiwi slices.

Variations There are many ways to make this bowlful of goodness. Substitute the açai purée for 5 frozen strawberries and top with extra strawberries and cacao nibs, or use 30 g/¼ cup frozen blueberries instead of the açai purée and top with sliced kiwi and coconut chips. For an extra-thick fruit base, add an extra frozen banana, or try blending in 2 teaspoons of cacao powder, then top with almond butter and hemp seeds for a chocolate and nut variation.

Other fun toppings include a handful of grain-free granola, a dollop of coconut yogurt, crushed seeds and nuts, or any sliced fruit you desire.

GRANOLA

125 ml/½ cup pure maple syrup
125 ml/½ cup agave syrup
200 ml/¾ cup flavourless oil,
   e.g. sunflower
2 teaspoons ground cinnamon
800 g/6½ cups jumbo oats
200 g/1½ cups mixed nuts and seeds
   e.g. pecans, hazelnuts, cashews
   and pumpkin seeds
150 g/1 cup raisins
150 g/1 cup chopped unsulphured
   dried apricots

Serves 10–12

Granola is absolutely one of the simplest things you can make in a kitchen, plus it costs half the price and tastes infinitely better than storebought.

Preheat the oven to 180°C (350°F) Gas 4.

Mix together the maple and agave syrups, oil and cinnamon. In a large mixing bowl, combine the oats and oil mixture until all the oats are evenly coated.

Spread the oats out on 2 baking sheets and bake in the preheated oven for about 20–30 minutes until they turn a lovely golden brown. Give them a stir once or twice during cooking to make sure they are all evenly cooked. If it looks like they might be burning, turn the oven temperature down slightly and stir them again.

While the oats are in the oven, you can also roast the mixed nuts and seeds for 10–15 minutes or until they go a shade darker and their flavours are released.

Let the oats and nuts cool down, then mix together with the raisins and apricots. If you feel like you want more cinnamon feel free to add more at this stage.

BIRCHER MUESLI

300 g/2½ cups jumbo oats
150 g/1 cup mixed seeds, e.g. pumpkin,
   sunflower, flaxseed etc.
2 apples, cored and grated
175 ml/⅔ cup rice milk
175 ml/⅔ cup apple or orange juice
100 g/⅔ cup raisins
50 g/⅓ cup dried cranberries
80 ml/⅓ cup pure maple or agave syrup
1–2 teaspoons ground cinnamon
400 ml/1¾ cups soy yogurt

Serves 4

Whether cooked for porridge or soaked and served with yogurt, oats are a breakfast mainstay. Served at room temperature, muesli is the perfect choice for summer mornings when you are in less need of warming porridge.

In a large bowl, mix together all the ingredients apart from the yogurt. Allow to soak for at least 1 hour until the oats have softened, or overnight. The mixture will thicken up considerably once soaked.

When ready to eat, taste and add more maple or agave syrup and cinnamon if required. Serve it up with as much yogurt as you like alongside it. You can mix it altogether for a looser bircher or you can dip into it as you please for a thicker consistency.

The wonderful thing about bircher muesli is that you can add whichever nuts, seeds and fruit you like, so you can really make it your own.

CINNAMON SPICED BRUSCHETTA
WITH BROWN SUGAR PLUMS

Sticky, cinnamon-spiced plums and crisp, oven-baked bruschetta make a truly exquisite start to the day. A cascade of coconut or soy milk yogurt, or even a cashew nut cream, lifts it right to the top of the ladder of loveliness.

600 g/21 oz. plums
4 medium slices rye sourdough bread
50 g/3½ tablespoons coconut oil
50 g/¼ cup dark or light muscovado sugar
1 teaspoon ground cinnamon

Serves 4

Preheat the oven to 200°C (400°F) Gas 6.

Cut the plums in half and remove the stones/pits. Arrange the plums, cut-side up, along one side of a baking sheet. Spread the bread with about half of the coconut oil. Dot the remaining oil over the plums. Mix the sugar and cinnamon together, sprinkle a little over each of the slices of bread and lay them on the other side of the baking sheet. Scatter the remaining cinnamon sugar over the plums. Bake for about 30 minutes, until the bread is crisp and the plums are beautifully soft. Pile the plums onto the bruschetta and serve warm, with coconut or soy yogurt.

SWEET TAHINI 'BUTTER'

If you love starting your day with toast, butter and jam, you have to try this!

4 tablespoons soy or oat cream
4 tablespoons white tahini
2–4 tablespoons rice or agave syrup
½ teaspoon pure vanilla extract
pinch of salt
4–5 slices of wholegrain bread,
    freshly toasted
4 tablespoons fruit jam/preserves
    or slices of fresh fruit, to serve

Serves 2

In a small saucepan, slowly heat the cream to a gentle simmer, then remove from the heat and add the tahini, syrup, vanilla and salt. Whisk until smooth – the consistency should be thick enough to be easily spread over slices of toast.

Cover each slice of toast with the spread, then top with jam/preserves of your choice, sliced fresh fruit or any other topping you like (dried fruits, chopped nuts, etc.). Serve for breakfast or as an afternoon snack with a cup of hot grain coffee or tea.

SMASHED AVOCADO ON TOAST
WITH RAW COURGETTE & HERB SALAD & DUKKAH

The dukkah adds texture and saltiness to the creaminess of the avocado
and the courgette/zucchini gives it a freshness.

2 ripe avocados
1 tablespoon freshly squeezed
   lemon juice
1 small courgette/zucchini
   (approx. 100 g/3½ oz.)
15 g/½ oz. mixed fresh herb leaves,
   such as mint, coriander/cilantro
   and flat-leaf parsley
2 teaspoons extra virgin olive oil
1 teaspoon grated lemon zest
2 slices of sourdough bread, toasted
2 tablespoons Dukkah (see below)
sea salt and freshly ground
   black pepper

Serves 2

DUKKAH
100 g/1 cup whole hazelnuts
20 g/¼ cup pistachio nuts
2 tablespoons coriander seeds
1 tablespoon cumin seeds
5 tablespooons sesame seeds
2 teaspoons white or
   black peppercorns
½ teaspoon dried chilli/
   hot red pepper flakes
½ teaspoon sea salt

Serves 4

Preheat the oven to 160°C (325°F) Gas 3.

For the dukkah, put the hazelnuts and pistachio nuts on separate baking sheets and roast in the preheated oven for 10 minutes. Remove from the oven and wrap the hazelnuts in a clean kitchen towel. Set aside for 1 minute then rub within the towel to remove the skins. When cool, roughly crush the nuts using a pestle and mortar. Transfer to a large bowl.

Put the coriander and cumin seeds in a preheated dry frying pan/skillet set over a medium heat. Dry-fry the seeds for couple of minutes, shaking the pan from time to time, until they start to pop. Remove the seeds from the pan and crush using a pestle and mortar. Add to the nut mixture. Repeat with the peppercorns.

Grind the chilli/hot red pepper flakes using the pestle and mortar and add to the nut and seed mixture. Finally, add the salt and mix everything together. This can be stored in an airtight container for up to 2 weeks.

Cut the avocados in half, remove the stones/pits and scoop out the flesh into a bowl. Roughly mash the flesh with a fork, keeping it quite chunky. Add the lemon juice with a generous pinch of sea salt and black pepper. Gently combine.

To make the courgette/zucchini salad, use a mandoline or vegetable peeler to slice the courgette/zucchini into long thin ribbons. Place into a bowl with the herb leaves, olive oil, lemon zest and a pinch of salt and pepper. Toss together.

Spread the smashed avocado generously onto the two slices of toast. Heap the courgette/zucchini salad on top and sprinkle with the dukkah.

DAIRY-FREE COCONUT PANCAKES
WITH LIME SYRUP & MANGO

These pancakes are completely dairy-free and egg-free. This makes them a bit more dense, but as they are served drenched in a lime syrup, this is soon taken care of. Try to find the ripest, most perfumed mango you can to make this dish exquisite.

150 g/1 cup plus 2 tablespoons
   plain/all-purpose flour
1 tablespoon baking powder
1/4 teaspoon salt
2 tablespoons demerara/
   turbinado sugar
3 tablespoons desiccated/
   dried unsweetened shredded
   coconut
200 ml/generous 3/4 cup coconut milk
2 tablespoons sunflower oil,
   plus extra for frying
1 mango, peeled, pitted and sliced,
   to serve

LIME SYRUP
freshly squeezed juice of 3 limes
grated zest of 1 lime
100 g/6 tablespoons agave syrup
6 cardamom pods, crushed

Serves 4

To make the lime syrup, put the lime juice and zest, syrup and cardamom pods in a small saucepan and bring to the boil. Boil for 5 minutes, then remove from the heat and set aside.

Meanwhile, for the pancake batter, sift the flour, baking powder and salt into a large mixing bowl and stir in the sugar and desiccated/dried shredded coconut. Put the coconut milk, 75 ml/1/3 cup water and the oil into a jug/pitcher and beat to combine. Mix the wet ingredients with the dry ingredients until no lumps of flour remain.

Heat a frying pan/skillet over a medium heat. Grease the pan with a paper towel dipped in oil. Drop 2–3 tablespoons of batter into the pan. Cook the pancakes for 1–2 minutes on each side until golden and cooked through. Remove the pancakes from the pan and keep them warm while you cook the remaining batter in the same way.

Serve the pancakes with slices of fresh mango and the lime syrup.

SOCCA PANCAKES
WITH ROASTED PEARS & TAHINI DRIZZLE

Socca are gluten-free pancakes made with protein-rich chickpea (gram) flour which makes them extra satisfying. This pear and maple-tahini topping is also good served with coconut yogurt, dairy-free ice cream or waffles. Both the pears and the sauce can be made in advance and the pears can be warmed up before topping the socca.

PANCAKE BATTER
125 g/1 cup minus 1 tablespoon chickpea (gram) flour
½ teaspoon salt
olive oil, for frying

ROASTED PEARS
melted coconut oil, for brushing
2 firm pears (such as Bosc) cored and sliced lengthways into 5 mm/¼-in. thick slices
¼ teaspoon ground cinnamon, plus more if needed

MAPLE-TAHINI DRIZZLE
60 g/¼ cup tahini
60 ml/¼ cup almond milk
1–2 tablespoons maple syrup
¼ teaspoon ground cinnamon
¼ teaspoon vanilla extract

baking sheet, lined with baking parchment

Serves 2

For the pancake batter, put the chickpea (gram) flour, salt and 295 ml/1¼ cups water into a large bowl and mix together with a whisk or a fork until well combined into a smooth batter. Leave to stand at room temperature for at least 10 minutes.

Preheat the oven to 180°C (350°F) Gas 4.

For the roasted pears, brush the baking parchment on the baking sheet with melted coconut oil and arrange the pear slices on top in a single layer. Brush the pears with more melted coconut oil and then sprinkle with cinnamon. Bake in the preheated oven for 30–40 minutes, flipping them at the 20-minute mark, until the pears have softened and are beginning to turn golden.

Meanwhile, prepare the maple-tahini drizzle. In a small bowl or jar, combine the tahini, almond milk, maple syrup, cinnamon and vanilla. Whisk by hand or use a stick blender to blend together until smooth.

Heat a little olive oil in another small frying pan/skillet over a medium heat. Add approximately 60–75 ml/¼–scant ⅓ cup of the socca batter to the warm pan. Swirl it around so that it covers the base of the pan. Fry for about 2–3 minutes, until the batter begins to form bubbles. Flip the pancake with a spatula and cook for another 1–2 minutes on the other side. Remove the pancake from the pan as soon as it is ready and keep warm while you cook the remaining batter in the same way. This should make you about four small socca pancakes in total.

Top the warm socca pancakes with the maple-tahini drizzle and pears and serve.

CRUSHED BUTTER BEANS
WITH ROASTED TOMATOES & AVOCADO

This dish is fabulous with crusty bread or sourdough toast for scooping up, and far better than any beans on toast you've ever tasted! It makes a perfect brunch dish, and an easy way to feed friends or family when you fancy something hot and tasty. It works well for lunch too.

600 g/21 oz. cherry tomatoes
4 tablespoons olive oil
3–4 leeks, trimmed and sliced
1 garlic clove, finely chopped
400-g/14-oz. can butter/
    lima beans, drained and rinsed
bunch of parsley, coarsely chopped
2 ripe but firm avocados
chilli/chile oil (optional)
paprika, to sprinkle
parsley leaves, to garnish

Serves 4

Preheat the oven to 180°C (350°F) Gas 4.

Scatter the cherry tomatoes over a large sheet pan and drizzle the olive oil over. Add the leeks and garlic and toss everything together. Roast for 20 minutes. Remove the sheet pan from the oven and scatter the butter/lima beans evenly over the tomatoes. Crush the beans lightly using the tines of a fork. Scatter over the chopped parsley. Return to the oven for a further 5 minutes.

Remove from the oven. Cut the avocados in half, remove the stones/pits and scoop out the flesh. Arrange evenly over the beans and tomatoes. Drizzle with chilli/chile oil (if using), add a light sprinkling of paprika and garnish with parsley leaves.

GRILLED TEMPEH BAGUETTE

Tempeh, the fermented soy product rich in protein and full of taste, is a great ingredient to use to veganize versions of hearty meat dishes. In this recipe, to give it even more oomph, thin tempeh slices are marinated in a tahini-enriched marinade and then grilled/broiled – the achieved texture is similar to that of crispy pancetta.

200-g/7-oz. block of tempeh
4 tablespoons tamari soy sauce
3 tablespoons tahini
1 teaspoon smoked paprika
1 teaspoon barbecue spice mix
1/4 teaspoon chilli/chili powder
2 tablespoons toasted sesame oil
1/2 teaspoon garlic powder
1/4 teaspoon crushed black pepper

TO SERVE
30-cm/12-in. French baguette
60 ml/1/4 cup vegan mayo
1 ripe avocado
6 big leaves of Romaine lettuce,
    or other greens
9 slices of large ripe tomatoes,
    deseeded
3 tablespoons sauerkraut
    or thinly sliced pickles
baking sheets lined with aluminium foil

Serves 3

Preheat the oven to 200°C (400°F) on grill/broiler mode or preheat the grill/broiler to high.

Cut the tempeh into thin slices – depending on the shape of the tempeh block, you should get 20–26 slices. In a bowl, whisk together all the other ingredients to make a smooth marinade.

Place the slices of tempeh on the prepared baking sheet. Cover each slice with the marinade, spreading it to cover the entire slice. Turn them over and do the same on the other side of each slice. Place the baking sheet in the upper part of the oven. Grill/broil for 8–10 minutes, checking occasionally – if you have a powerful oven, the slices could be ready faster. Turn the tempeh slices and grill/broil again until the marinade is soaked in and the slices are crispy and golden brown.

Cut the baguette in half lengthways and lightly toast.

Peel, stone/pit and slice the avocado. Spread some dressing or mayo on both halves of the baguette. Layer the bottom half with slices of tomato and sauerkraut or pickles. Add the tempeh slices, then top with slices of avocado and greens. Cover with the top half of the baguette. Slice across into three same-sized sandwiches with a sharp bread knife and serve immediately. If there are any leftover fillings, serve them on the side.

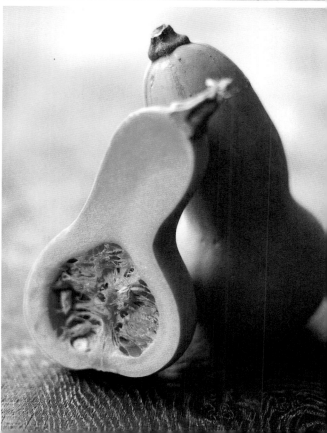

LIGHT BITES
& SNACKS

HOT SPINACH & ARTICHOKE DIP

1 x 390-g/14-oz. can artichokes
30 g/³/₄ cup macadamia nuts
200 ml/³/₄ cup non-dairy milk
   (such as almond, soy, or coconut milk)
½ tablespoon salt
2 garlic cloves
3 tablespoons nutritional yeast
½ white onion, diced
olive oil, for sautéing
½ tablespoon arrowroot starch
400 g/8 cups spinach
dried chilli/hot red pepper flakes
   (optional)
crudités, to serve
6 ceramic ramekins

Serves 6

You might find that when you start eating this dip, you just can't stop. With this version there's no reason to stop – it's all good stuff – so enjoy!

Preheat your oven to 200°C (400°F) Gas 6.

Cut the artichokes into small bite-sized pieces and set aside. Put the macadamia nuts, non-dairy milk, salt, garlic and nutritional yeast in a high-speed blender and blend until completely smooth.

Sauté the onion in a little olive oil in a large frying pan/skillet set over a medium heat. Once browned, pour in the macadamia nut mixture and stir in the arrowroot. The mixture will start to thicken. Divide the spinach and artichokes between your ramekins and pour some of the warm macadamia mixture over the vegetables. Sprinkle each ramekin with dried chilli/hot red pepper flakes, if using. Place the filled ramekins on a baking sheet and bake in the preheated oven for about 18 minutes, or until the tops have hardened. Serve immediately with your choice of crudités. These are best eaten warm but can be kept for up to 4 days in the fridge.

CHAPATIS

This is a great dipper, especially for Indian-spiced dishes. In case you're avoiding yeasty breads, chapatis are a great alternative, and so easy to make!

150 g/1 cup wholemeal/
   whole-wheat flour, plus extra for dusting
150 g/1 cup unbleached plain/all-purpose
   flour, plus extra for dusting
½ teaspoon sea salt
140 ml/generous ½ cup lukewarm water
2 tablespoons sesame or olive oil

*Makes 10 chapatis,
13 cm/5-in. in diameter*

Put both flours in a bowl. Add the salt and oil, and whisk to combine. Gradually add the water and knead to form a smooth, medium-soft dough. Cover with a damp kitchen towel and set aside for 15 minutes to rest.

Divide the dough into 10 equal portions and form each portion into a ball, rolling them until smooth and without cracks. Coat each ball in flour and roll out into chapatis, 13 cm/5 inches in diameter, with the help of a rolling pin. Lightly coat each chapati in flour on both sides to prevent from sticking. Heat a cast-iron or stainless-steel pan over a medium heat and start frying. The chapati is ready for turning when bumps appear on its surface, but it shouldn't brown. Turn it onto the other side and flip again once the bumps appear. After the second flip, leave it in the pan for a moment, and then gently press the chapati around its edges with a kitchen towel or oven mitt. It should puff up in the middle. Continue with the remaining chapatis. Serve.

RYE CRACKERS WITH CHIA SEEDS

These homemade crackers spread with hummus and topped with raw or fermented veggies are the perfect snack for munching your worries away!

130 g/³/₄ cup rye flour

130 g/³/₄ cup unbleached plain/
    all-purpose flour

15 g/2 tablespoons chia seeds

4 g/scant 1 teaspoon salt

freshly ground black pepper, to taste

60 ml/¹/₄ cup olive oil or light
    sesame oil

60 ml/¹/₄ cup water

1 teaspoon dark agave
    or maple syrup

hummus, cucumber and micro cress,
    to serve (optional)

*baking sheet, lined with
    baking parchment*

*Makes 12–16
crackers*

Combine all the dry ingredients in a large bowl. Emulsify all the wet ingredients with a whisk, and then slowly add them to the flour and seed mixture, stirring until well combined. The dough should quickly form a ball and shouldn't be sticky. Knead a couple of times; just enough to make sure all the ingredients are evenly distributed. Wrap in clingfilm/plastic wrap or cover with a damp kitchen towel and let sit at room temperature for 10 minutes. Resting the dough makes rolling it out much easier.

Preheat the oven to 200°C (400°F) Gas 6.

Divide the dough into three equal pieces. Roll out a very thin layer of dough between two sheets of baking parchment. If you like really crunchy crackers, the dough should be almost paper-thin, but if you like a bit of texture, roll to desired thickness.

Use a knife or pizza cutter to cut out shapes. Squares or rectangles are practical choices, since you'll have not much leftover dough. Transfer the crackers to the lined baking sheet using a thin spatula or a knife. Prick each a couple of times with a fork.

Bake for 4–7 minutes, depending on the thickness of the crackers. Remember, they shouldn't brown, just get slightly golden. They will firm up as they cool, so don't expect them to be cracker-crunchy straight out of the oven.

Here, they are spread with hummus and topped with cucumber and micro cress, but you can eat them how you prefer! Store in an air-tight container after they've cooled completely.

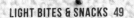

GRAIN-FREE 'CHEESY' PUMPKIN CRACKERS

90 g/3¼ oz. pumpkin seeds
2 large garlic cloves, skins peeled
10 g/¼ oz. poppy seeds or
　flaxseeds/linseeds
½ teaspoon sea salt
15 g/½ oz. nutritional yeast flakes
1½ teaspoons caraway seeds
1 tablespoon extra virgin olive oil
50 ml/3½ tablespoons water
freshly ground black pepper
baking sheet, lined with baking parchment

Makes 16

Nutritional yeast flakes don't sound particularly appetizing, but they are nutritionally abundant and have a distinctly cheesy flavour.

Preheat the oven to 190°C (375°F) Gas 5.

Put the pumpkin seeds and garlic in a food processor and process to a coarse paste. Add the rest of the ingredients, season with pepper and blend until the mixture starts to come together in a ball of dough.

Form the dough into a flattened rectangle and place between two sheets of baking parchment. Using a rolling pin, roll the dough into a thin rectangle, about 3 mm/⅛ inch thick and mark the dough into 16 5-cm/2-inch squares with the pointed-end of a knife. Place on the lined baking sheet and bake for about 20–25 minutes until light golden and firm.

Using the marked lines, cut into 16 squares and remove from the baking sheet, using the baking parchment to help you. Leave to cool on a wire rack and then separate into individual crackers. Store in an airtight container for 3–5 days.

CAJUN TORTILLA CHIPS

4 corn tortillas
½ teaspoon spirulina powder (optional)
1 teaspoon sesame seeds
extra virgin olive oil, for brushing

CAJUN SPICE MIX
1 teaspoon dried oregano
1 tablespoon paprika
2 teaspoons ground turmeric
½ teaspoon chilli/chili powder
2 teaspoons ground cumin
1 teaspoon garlic granules/powder

Serves 4

Super-easy corn chips without the usual additives and flavourings, which are often found in shop-bought versions. You'll have leftovers of the Cajun spice mix, but it keeps well in a lidded jar for a couple of months or so.

Preheat the oven to 180°C (350°F) Gas 4.

Mix together all the ingredients for the Cajun spice mix.

Place the tortillas directly on the shelves in the oven, spacing them apart so they don't touch each other. Bake for about 8 minutes, turning once, until crisp and golden in places. Remove from the oven and place on a wire rack.

Brush one side of each tortilla with oil and sprinkle over ¼ teaspoon of the Cajun spice mix, as well as the spirulina, if using, and some sesame seeds. Cut into wedges, then leave to cool and crisp up. They will keep in an airtight container for up to 2 days.

CARAMELIZED CARROT HUMMUS

Carrots are a sweet root vegetable, and you can emphasize that sweetness even more by long, slow sautéing in oil. Rosemary gives a Mediterranean touch to the combination.

4 carrots
5 tablespoons light sesame oil or olive oil, plus a little extra to serve
1/4 teaspoon coarse sea salt
2 sprigs of rosemary or 2 teaspoons dried rosemary needles
1 tablespoon soy sauce
1 tablespoon dark agave nectar
1 quantity hummus (see page 17, but omit the olive oil since we're adding oil to the carrots)

Makes 3–5 servings

Wash and scrub the carrots, then cut into large bite-size pieces (Chinese 'rolling-style' cutting technique is the best choice for this dish). Heat the oil in a cast-iron wok or stainless-steel heavy-bottomed pan, over a medium heat. Add the carrots and sprinkle with the coarse sea salt. Stir well, coating all the carrot pieces in oil. Once they start sizzling, lower the heat, add the rosemary sprigs/needles and sauté for at least 20 minutes, or longer, stirring constantly to avoid burning the carrots.

The carrots are ready when they shrink to half of their original size, and become very soft and fragrant. At the end of sautéing, add the soy sauce and agave, and stir quickly over a high heat until absorbed.

Two options to serve: you can either blend the carrots into the hummus, or just stir the caramelized carrots into the hummus and serve.

Other root vegetables such as parsnip, parsley root, celeriac/celery root and even sweet potato can be caramelized this way. Try adding other spices of choice, too!

CHILLI-CHEESE BUTTERNUT SQUASH FRIES

These 'fries' have the benefit of being baked rather than fried, which not only reduces the calorie count but also cuts out the carcinogenic trans-fats that the frying process creates.

1 butternut squash, peeled
1 small red chilli/chile
4 tablespoons cashew butter
1 tablespoon olive oil
1 teaspoon salt
2 tablespoons nutritional yeast
sweet and spicy sauce (try Frank's hot sauce), to serve

baking sheet, greased and lined with baking parchment

Serves 4

Preheat the oven to 220°C (425°F) Gas 7.

Slice the butternut squash into thick batons and set aside.

Thinly slice the red chilli/chile into small pieces, discarding the seeds (unless you want the fries super spicy!), and mix together with the cashew butter, olive oil and salt in a large mixing bowl.

Add the fries to the mixture and toss to coat, then dip each one in the nutritional yeast. Transfer to the prepared baking sheet and bake in the preheated oven for 40 minutes, turning halfway through cooking. Remove from the oven and serve with sweet and spicy sauce.

CAPONATA

In Italy caponata is enjoyed as a warm vegetable side dish or as part of a cold vegetable antipasto. This take on the classic Sicilian recipe is best enjoyed at room temperature as a dip with toasted ciabatta. It keeps well so can be made ahead and enjoyed the next day.

1 aubergine/eggplant, cubed
1 teaspoon ground cinnamon
2 tablespoons olive oil
1 red onion, chopped
2 celery stalks, sliced
1 garlic clove, crushed
400-g/14-oz. can chopped tomatoes
handful of sultanas/golden raisins
2 tablespoons white wine
2 teaspoons capers, drained
1 tablespoon white wine vinegar
2 teaspoons sugar
squeeze of fresh lemon juice
sea salt and freshly ground
    black pepper

TO SERVE
handful of freshly chopped flat-leaf
    parsley leaves
drizzle of extra virgin olive oil
freshly squeezed lemon juice
slices of ciabatta, toasted

Serves 4–6

Season the aubergine/eggplant cubes generously with salt and pepper, and sprinkle with cinnamon. Heat the olive oil in a large frying pan/skillet set over a low heat, add the aubergine/eggplant and cook for about 10 minutes until soft and starting to turn golden. Remove the aubergine/eggplant from the pan and set aside until needed.

Return the pan to the heat and add the onion, celery and garlic, and cook for about 8 minutes until the vegetables begin to soften. Add the tomatoes, sultanas/golden raisins and white wine, and simmer over a low heat for about 20 minutes. Stir in the cooked aubergine/eggplant, add the capers, vinegar, sugar and lemon juice, and cook over a low heat until the taste of vinegar softens. Remove from the heat and allow to cool to room temperature.

To serve, stir in the parsley and add a drizzle of olive oil and a squeeze of lemon juice. Spoon onto slices of toasted ciabatta.

STUFFED COURGETTES/ZUCCHINI

500 g/1 large courgette/zucchini
1 tablespoon olive oil
60 g/1 medium onion, chopped
¼ teaspoon ground turmeric
½ teaspoon oregano
1 tablespoon tomato purée/paste (optional)
1 tablespoon tamari soy sauce
130 g/¾ cup cooked barley (or other grains)
2 tablespoons freshly chopped
    parsley leaves
100 g/½ cup leftover hummus
sea salt
purple basil, to garnish
mixed salad leaves, drizzled with
    lemon juice, to serve
baking sheets, lined with baking parchment

Serves 4

A great go-to courgette/zucchini recipe. Feel free to use up any leftover cooked grains you might have in the fridge.

Preheat the oven to 180°C (350°F) Gas 4.

Wash and cut the courgette/zucchini into three equal pieces crossways. Cut each piece in half lengthways. With a sharp spoon or knife, scoop out the seeds, making space for the filling. Save the scooped flesh to use for a soup or stew. Brush each courgette/zucchini piece with the olive oil and season with a pinch of salt.

In a heavy-bottomed pan over a medium heat, dry-fry the chopped onion with a pinch of salt, stirring often. Add the turmeric, oregano, tomato purée/paste and tamari, and stir until fragrant and browned. Add the cooked barley, parsley and hummus, and stir well until incorporated.

Place the courgette/zucchini pieces on the prepared baking sheet and divide the stuffing amongst them. Bake in the preheated oven for 20 minutes or until the courgette/zucchini flesh gets slightly soft. Garnish with purple basil and serve with mixed salad leaves drizzled with lemon juice.

NOT-YOUR-AVERAGE WRAP

2 large chard leaves
1 large papaya (or 2 small papayas),
    peeled and sliced
1 mango, peeled, stoned/pitted and sliced
2 avocados, peeled, stoned/pitted
    and sliced
large handful of alfalfa sprouts
small handful of beansprouts
6 tablespoons crushed almonds,
    (or other nut of choice),
    plus 1 tablespoon, for topping
MISO-SESAME DRESSING
2 teaspoons brown miso paste
2 tablespoons toasted sesame oil

Serves 2

Chard is nature's way of giving us the convenience of a sandwich, all contained and no clean-up necessary, without the need for refined carbohydrates. You can pretty much use chard as a wrap for any of your favourite sandwich fillings.

Using a sharp knife, lay your chard leaves out flat and cut in half down the middle, discarding the stems completely.

Place a quarter of the papaya, mango, avocado, alfalfa sprouts and beansprouts down the middle of each halved chard leaf. Sprinkle the nuts over the mixture and roll the chard leaf around the mixture as you would for a sandwich wrap.

For the dressing, whisk the miso paste and sesame oil together in a small mixing bowl. Pour over the top of the chard wraps, sprinkle with extra crushed nuts and serve immediately.

SEED FALAFEL

Here's a fry-free and chickpea-free falafel that's surprisingly easy to make. It's also a great lunchbox item and the mix can stay fresh in the fridge for days. These green balls go with just about anything — in salads, with cooked vegetables, alongside soups or as an appetizer. It's a great way to introduce more seeds into your diet!

130 g/1 cup pumpkin seeds
130 g/1 cup sunflower seeds
50 g/½ cup walnuts
5 tablespoons freshly chopped
    flat-leaf parsley
5 dried tomato halves, soaked
2 garlic cloves, crushed
3 tablespoons olive oil
freshly squeezed juice of ½ lemon
1 teaspoon dried oregano
1 tablespoon water, if necessary
sea salt and freshly ground
    black pepper

Makes 24

Grind the seeds in a food processor or blender into a fine flour, making sure you don't process them for too long, otherwise they might turn into seed butter. Finely chop the walnuts, as they'll give the falafels a nice crunchy texture. Add them, together with the remaining ingredients, (except the water) to the seed flour and mix well with your hands or with a silicone spatula. Taste and adjust the seasoning if necessary – it should taste strong and full of flavour. Try squeezing the seed mixture in your hand and if it doesn't fall apart it's moist enough. In case it feels dry and crumbles immediately, add the water and mix again.

Form the mixture into walnut-sized falafel balls and either serve them up or keep them refrigerated before use.

SOUPS
& SIDES

LENTIL & SQUASH SOUP

1 large onion, finely chopped
2 teaspoons sea salt
2 tablespoons vegetable oil
2 garlic cloves, chopped
1 teaspoon chopped fresh ginger
2 teaspoons ground cumin
1 teaspoon chilli/chili powder
1 teaspoon ground turmeric
2 teaspoons ground coriander
350 g/2 cups red lentils
1.4 litres/6 cups water
500 ml/2 cups vegetable stock
500 g/3 cups chopped butternut squash
2 tablespoons flaxseed oil
handful of fresh coriander/cilantro,
    to garnish

Serves 8–10

Red lentils are quick to cook, tasty, and easy to digest. Red lentils and squash marry well with Indian spices. Spices like turmeric, ginger and coriander are great for digestive health. You might like to make a big batch of this soup as it freezes really well.

In a large saucepan or pot, fry the onion and salt in vegetable oil until the onion is soft. Add the garlic, ginger and spices and fry for about 1 minute.

Put the lentils in the bottom of the pan and coat them with the spice mixture. Add the water, vegetable stock and squash and bring to the boil. Reduce the heat, cover and simmer for about 20–30 minutes. Set aside to cool slightly.

Once cooled, purée the soup in a food processor, add the flaxseed oil and adjust the seasoning as required. Return to the heat and warm through.

Serve in bowls and garnish with fresh coriander/cilantro. The soup can be stored in the freezer for up to 3 months.

GREEN ENERGY SOUP

3 kale leaves, de-stalked
15-cm/6-in. piece of cucumber
1/2 red (bell) pepper
1 teaspoon grated fresh ginger
freshly squeezed juice of 1 lemon
1 avocado, peeled and stoned/pitted
250 ml/1 cup coconut water
1 tomato, halved
4 tablespoons freshly chopped dill,
    plus extra to serve
1 garlic clove
1/4 onion
1/2 teaspoon salt
olive oil, to serve
freshly ground black pepper, to serve
a high-speed blender

Serves 2

Fresh soups are the ultimate light lunch and a super-healthy option. Store-bought varieties are often loaded with cream, excessive amounts of salt, and inevitably, tonnes of preservatives in order for them to survive on the shelf, so avoid them if you can. If you love soup and want all the benefits of the easy-to-assimilate nutrients, whizzing this up at home will take less time than it takes to run out and buy one.

Put all of the ingredients in a blender and blitz on a low speed until completely smooth.

Transfer the mixture to a small saucepan or pot set over a medium heat and warm through.

Pour into serving bowls, drizzle with olive oil, sprinkle with black pepper and a few extra sprigs of dill, and serve immediately.

HEARTY MISO SOUP

Don't forget squashes and pumpkins! They're not only tasty and nourishing but also have a lot of beta-carotene – one of the most important antioxidants. However, the same applies to carrots, if you don't have a pumpkin at hand! This is a great soup to warm you up, at the same time feeding your body with vital enzymes from the miso paste.

2 tablespoons dark sesame oil
60 g/½ cup diced onion
60 g /½ cup peeled, seeded and cubed pumpkin, squash or carrots
4 garlic cloves, crushed
1 tablespoon crushed fresh ginger
800 ml/3½ cups cold water or bouillon (unsalted)
1 tablespoon barley or rice miso
¼ sheet toasted nori, cut into small pieces
1 tablespoon freshly chopped flat-leaf parsley
1 teaspoon toasted sesame seeds
sea salt

Serves 2-3

In a large saucepan, sauté the onion for a minute or so in the sesame oil, before adding pumpkin, squash or carrot, along with the garlic, ginger and a pinch of salt. Sauté the mixture for a little longer, and then add the cold water or bouillon and cover. Bring to a boil, lower the heat and cook until the vegetables become tender.

Take 60 ml/¼ cup of the hot soup and put it in a small bowl. Now add the tablespoon of miso to it. Purée the miso really well with a fork, until it has completely melted. Put the miso liquid back into the soup. Taste and adjust the seasoning. Turn off the heat, cover and let the soup sit for a couple of minutes. Serve sprinkled with the pieces of nori, the chopped parsley and sesame seeds.

Don't forget that you can combine different kinds of miso in the same soup! Since hatcho (soya/soy bean) miso is of high quality but has a strong taste, try to combine ½ tablespoon soya/soy miso with ½ tablespoon barley miso, to get all the benefits of both kinds of soya/soy bean paste. In warmer weather, substitute darker miso pastes with sweet white miso, which is a lot milder.

QUINOA SOUP WITH RED BEANS AND KALE

This is a great take on a Southern Cajun soup, using the superfoods kale and quinoa. Taking the step to purée some of the beans and stock is necessary to get the perfect consistency but if you're short on time, substitute kidney beans from a jar.

175 g/1 cup dried red kidney beans
1 onion, chopped
1 green (bell) pepper, chopped
2 celery stalks, chopped
2 tablespoons olive oil
2 garlic cloves, finely chopped
300 ml/1¼ cups vegetable stock
750 ml/3 cups water
160 g/¾ cup quinoa
2 teaspoons dried oregano
pinch of cayenne pepper
2 teaspoons paprika
100 g/1 large bunch kale
sea salt and freshly ground
   black pepper

Serves 4–6

Put the dry red kidney beans in a bowl and soak in water overnight. When you are ready to make the soup, drain and set aside.

In a large saucepan or pot, heat the onion, green pepper and celery in oil over a medium heat. Cook for about 3 minutes or until the onion is translucent. Then add the garlic, stir, and cook for another minute. Put the drained red kidney beans into the pan with the vegetable stock and water. Bring the liquid to a boil then reduce the heat, cover and simmer until the beans are tender. This usually takes around 50 minutes.

Remove 500 ml/2 cups of the stock and 2 teaspoons of the beans and purée in a food processor. Then return the thickened purée to the pan.

Now add the quinoa, herbs and spices. Return to the boil, then reduce the heat, cover and simmer for 15 minutes. Meanwhile, prepare the kale.

Wash the kale in cold water. Then trim the stems and roughly chop the leaves. After the quinoa has been cooking for 15 minutes, add the kale. Cover and continue to cook for another 8 minutes, until the quinoa is fully cooked.

Add salt and pepper to taste and serve immediately.

ROASTED ASPARAGUS & FARRO SOUP

Roasting asparagus gives this soup a depth of flavour that makes it extra special. For a gluten-free variation, replace the farro with brown rice or quinoa.

185 g/1 cup dried farro
750 ml/3 cups water
900 g/2 lb asparagus
2 small shallots, chopped
2 tablespoons olive oil
1 teaspoon Himalayan salt
1 teaspoon freshly ground
    black pepper
2 garlic cloves, crushed
1 litre/4 cups low sodium
    vegetable stock
1 teaspoon allspice
handful of fresh flat-leaf parsley
grated zest of 1 lemon
*2 large baking sheets lined with
    baking parchment*

Serves 4

Preheat the oven to 190°C (375°F) Gas 5.

Rinse the farro under cold, running water in a sieve/strainer. Put the farro and water in a large saucepan or pot on a high heat and bring to the boil. Reduce the heat, cover and simmer for 15 minutes, then drain and set aside.

Rinse and trim the asparagus, discarding the bottom ends of the asparagus. Lay on one of the prepared baking sheets with the shallots. Drizzle with oil, season well with salt and pepper, and add the garlic. Roast for 20 minutes, turning once.

Purée the cooked asparagus in two batches together with 500 ml/2 cups of vegetable stock in the first batch and the remainder in the second. Transfer the liquid to a saucepan or pot.

Bring the soup to a simmer over a high heat and stir in the allspice. Add a little extra water to reach the desired consistency if needed. Add the drained farro and season to taste.

Serve in bowls and garnish with fresh parsley and lemon zest.

SWEET POTATO & COCONUT SOUP
WITH THAI PESTO

1 tablespoon light olive oil
500 g/18 oz. sweet potato, peeled
    and chopped into chunks
1 red onion, chopped
1 tablespoon Thai red curry paste
500 ml/2 cups vegetable stock
500 ml/2 cups coconut milk

THAI PESTO
100 g/³/₄ cup unsalted peanuts,
    lightly toasted
2 garlic cloves, chopped
2 teaspoons finely grated
    fresh ginger
2 large green chillies/chiles,
    deseeded and chopped
small bunch of fresh coriander/
    cilantro
large handful of fresh mint leaves
large handful of fresh basil leaves
2 tablespoons light soy sauce
    or vegan fish sauce
2 tablespoons freshly squeezed
    lime juice
1 tablespoon soft light brown sugar

Serves 4

Sweet potatoes make an excellent ingredient for soups. When blended they take on a velvety, creamy texture. Here, their sweetness is cut through with some full-on and spicy Asian flavours in the form of a Thai-style pesto, which really brings this soup to life.

Put the oil in a heavy-based saucepan set over a medium heat. Add the sweet potato and onion, partially cover with a lid and cook for 15 minutes, stirring often, until they are soft and just starting to turn golden. Increase the heat to high, add the curry paste and stir-fry with the sweet potato for 3–4 minutes so that the paste cooks and becomes fragrant. Add the stock and coconut milk and bring to the boil. Transfer the mixture to a food processor or blender and whizz until smooth. Return the soup to a clean saucepan.

To make the pesto, put all of the ingredients in a food processor or blender and whizz, occasionally scraping down the sides of the bowl, until you have a chunky green paste and the ingredients are all evenly chopped.

Gently reheat the soup, then ladle into warmed serving bowls. Top with a generous spoonful of Thai pesto to serve.

FREEKEH, PUMPKIN & CRISPY GINGER SALAD

500 g/18 oz. pumpkin or butternut squash, peeled, seeded and cut into pieces
3 tablespoons olive oil
125 g/1 cup freekeh
3-cm/1¼-in. piece fresh root ginger, peeled and cut into thin strips
1 large onion, chopped
2 large garlic cloves, chopped
3 handfuls of sultanas/golden raisins

finely grated zest and freshly squeezed juice of 1 orange
1 teaspoon ground allspice
1 teaspoon ground ginger
squeeze of lemon juice
2 handfuls of freshly chopped coriander/cilantro leaves, plus a few whole leaves to decorate
sea salt and freshly ground black pepper

Serves 4

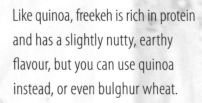

Like quinoa, freekeh is rich in protein and has a slightly nutty, earthy flavour, but you can use quinoa instead, or even bulghur wheat.

Preheat the oven to 200°C (400°F) Gas 6. Toss the pumpkin in 1 tablespoon of the oil and season, then spread out evenly in a large roasting pan. Roast for 30–35 minutes, turning once, until tender and starting to turn golden in places.

Meanwhile, put the freekeh in a pan and cover with water. Bring to the boil, then turn the heat down, cover and simmer for 15 minutes or until tender. Drain and transfer to a serving bowl.

Heat the remaining oil in a frying pan/skillet over a medium heat and fry the ginger for 3 minutes, until crisp and golden. Remove from the pan with a slotted spoon, drain on paper towels and set aside. Add the onion to the pan and fry for 8 minutes, stirring regularly, until softened. Add the garlic and cook for a further minute.

Stir the onion and garlic into the freekeh with the sultanas/golden raisins, orange zest and juice, allspice and ginger. Add a squeeze of lemon juice and the coriander/cilantro, season well, and stir until combined. Serve, sprinkled with the crispy ginger.

AMARANTH & GREEN LENTIL SALAD WITH ZA'ATAR

165 g/5½ oz. green lentils, rinsed
4 tablespoons amaranth
6 spring onions/scallions, thinly sliced
6 vine-ripened tomatoes, roughly chopped
1 yellow courgette/zucchini,
    coarsely grated
2 handfuls of freshly chopped mint leaves,
    plus a few whole leaves to decorate
1 tablespoon za'atar

DRESSING
2 tablespoons pomegranate molasses
3 tablespoons extra virgin olive oil
finely grated zest and freshly squeezed
    juice of 1 lemon
sea salt and freshly ground black pepper

Serves 4

This tiny grain (or, more accurately, seed) packs a powerful nutritional punch for its diminutive size. Popular in South America, amaranth is gluten-free as well as being a good source of digestible protein and valuable minerals. It is best mixed with other grains or pulses to give it a bit more substance.

Put the lentils in a large pan and cover with plenty of cold water. Bring to the boil, then turn the heat down and simmer, part-covered, for 20 minutes or until tender. Drain and transfer the lentils to a serving bowl.

Meanwhile, toast the amaranth in a dry pan for 2 minutes, shaking the pan regularly, until the grains start to pop and turn golden. Pour enough water over to cover and bring to the boil, then turn the heat down and simmer for 6 minutes or until tender. Drain and add to the bowl with the lentils.

Mix together all the dressing ingredients and season.

Add the spring onions/scallions, tomatoes, courgette/zucchini and mint to the serving bowl, and pour enough of the dressing over to coat. Toss until combined and serve, sprinkled with the za'atar and a few whole mint leaves.

RED QUINOA TABBOULEH

125 g/4¼ oz. red quinoa
6 vine-ripened tomatoes, quartered,
    seeded and chopped
2 small Lebanese cucumbers, quartered
    lengthways and diced
4 spring onions/scallions, finely chopped
1 courgette/zucchini, coarsely grated
6 tablespoons freshly chopped mint
6 tablespoons freshly chopped
    flat leaf parsley

DRESSING
3 tablespoons extra virgin olive oil
4 tablespoons freshly squeezed lemon juice
pinch of cumin seeds
sea salt and freshly ground black pepper

Serves 4

Quinoa makes a nutritious alternative to the more usual bulghur wheat in a tabbouleh. The secret to a successful tabbouleh is to get the right balance of grain to fresh produce; too much of the former makes for a slightly dull salad so be generous with the herbs and vegetables.

Put the quinoa in a pan and cover with water. Bring to the boil, then turn the heat down and simmer, covered, for 10–15 minutes until tender. Drain, transfer the quinoa to a serving bowl and leave to cool slightly.

Meanwhile, mix together all the ingredients for the dressing and season to taste.

Add the tomatoes, cucumbers, spring onions/scallions, courgette/zucchini and herbs to the quinoa. Pour the dressing over and toss to combine everything. Check the seasoning and serve at room temperature.

KAMUT WITH CHERMOULA DRESSING

400 g/14 oz. vine-ripened cherry tomatoes
1 tablespoon extra virgin olive oil
150 g/5 oz. kamut
200 g/7 oz. spring greens/collards or kale,
    tough outer leaves and stems discarded,
    leaves finely shredded
2 large handfuls of coriander/cilantro
    leaves, chopped

CHERMOULA DRESSING

1 small preserved lemon and 2 tablespoons
    juice from the jar
4 tablespoons extra virgin olive oil
2 garlic cloves, crushed
1 teaspoon each ground cumin,
    ground ginger and ground coriander
½ teaspoon dried chilli flakes/
    hot red pepper flakes
sea salt and freshly ground black pepper

Serves 4

Kamut, or khorasan wheat, is an ancient type of Middle Eastern wheat, which is experiencing a resurgence in popularity. This high-protein grain has a nutty flavour and keeps its texture after cooking, but you can use barley or rice instead, if you cannot get hold of it.

Preheat the oven to 200°C (400°F) Gas 6. Toss the tomatoes in the oil and spread out in a large roasting pan. Roast for 15–20 minutes, until starting to collapse.

Meanwhile, put the kamut in a pan and cover with plenty of water. Bring to the boil, then turn the heat down, part-cover and simmer for 10–12 minutes, until tender. Drain and transfer to a serving bowl with the spring greens/collards and coriander/cilantro.

For the dressing, scoop out and discard the flesh from the preserved lemon. Finely chop the skin and combine it with the rest of the ingredients in a bowl. Season. Spoon half of the dressing over the salad and toss to combine. Pile the tomatoes on top, then spoon over the rest of the dressing and serve.

SPICED CAULIFLOWER WITH RED PEPPER & PEAS

½ head of cauliflower, cut into large florets
2 teaspoons ground cumin
1 teaspoon ground turmeric
3 tablespoons light olive oil
2 teaspoons black mustard seeds
6–8 curry leaves
1 onion, sliced
1 small red (bell) pepper, thinly sliced
1 tablespoon finely grated fresh ginger
2 garlic cloves, chopped
1 large green chilli/chile, sliced
125 ml/½ cup vegetable stock
2 ripe tomatoes, chopped
125 g/4½ oz. freshly shelled peas
steamed or boiled basmati rice,
    to serve (optional)

Serves 4

The vegetarian recipes you find in Indian cuisine are some of the most delicious in the world. This dish embraces the philosophy of cooking fresh produce, keeping it simple and letting the flavours speak for themselves.

Put the cauliflower florets in a large bowl with the cumin and turmeric and toss until evenly coated in the spices.

Put the oil in a frying pan/skillet set over a medium/high heat. Add the cauliflower, mustard seeds and curry leaves and cook for 8–10 minutes, turning the pieces often so that they soften and colour with the spices. Add the onion and red (bell) pepper and cook for 5 minutes. Add the ginger, garlic and chilli/chile and stir-fry for 1 minute, then add the stock, tomatoes and peas. Reduce the heat and let simmer gently for 10 minutes until the vegetables are tender and cooked through.

Spoon over basmati rice to serve, if liked.

QUINOA TABBOULEH

150 g/³/₄ cup quinoa

4 vine-ripened tomatoes, peeled, deseeded and diced

2–3 tablespoons freshly chopped flat leaf parsley

2–3 tablespoons freshly chopped mint

½ red onion, very thinly sliced (optional)

6 spring onions/scallions, finely sliced

DRESSING

6 tablespoons extra virgin olive oil

freshly squeezed juice of 2 lemons

sea salt and freshly ground black pepper

Serves 6
as a side dish

Of course traditional tabbouleh is made with bulgur wheat. This version uses a pseudo-grain for reasons of nutrition and easier digestion. The quinoa works really well in this straightforward dish.

Place the quinoa in a sieve/strainer and rinse thoroughly. Put into a saucepan with 250 ml/1 cup of water.

Bring to the boil, then turn down the heat. Cover and leave to simmer for 15–20 minutes until the quinoa is tender and the water is absorbed. Transfer to a bowl and leave to cool.

Add the diced tomatoes to the quinoa, then stir in the parsley, mint, red onion (if using) and spring onions/scallions.

Whisk together all the ingredients for the dressing in a small bowl and season to taste. Pour over the tabbouleh. Stir, then serve.

WALDORF SALAD

50 g/½ cup walnuts

1 head butterhead lettuce

½ head radicchio

3 sticks celery, sliced

225 g/1½ cups red grapes, halved

1 green apple, cored and sliced

WALDORF DRESSING

1 avocado, peeled, stoned/pitted and roughly chopped

1 teaspoon English mustard

2 tablespoons white wine vinegar

Serves 2

This salad feels very elegant. Where the original was made with generous amounts of mayonnaise, the avocado-based dressing sneaks in extra nutrition.

Begin by toasting the walnuts in a dry frying pan/skillet set over a medium heat until they are crispy and browned. Remove from the heat and set aside (it's ok if you nibble on a few while you prepare the rest of the meal though!).

Tear off the larger leaves from the head of butterhead lettuce and layer them on the bottom of your plates or serving dish.

Chop the rest of the lettuce along with the radicchio and put it in a large mixing bowl. Add the sliced celery, grapes, apple and toasted walnuts.

To make the Waldorf dressing, mash the avocado in a small mixing bowl. Add the mustard and white wine vinegar and whisk to combine. Add 1–2 tablespoons of water to thin out the mixture, then add to the mixed salad. Toss until everything is well coated, then spoon the mixture onto the large butterhead lettuce leaves on your serving plates.

ROASTED VEGETABLE SALAD
WITH TAPENADE DRESSING

2 tablespoons extra virgin olive oil

2 tablespoons balsamic vinegar

8 baby courgettes/zucchini,
    halved lengthways

2 onions, halved and each half
    cut into 3 wedges

1 large red (bell) pepper, halved,
    deseeded and cut into
    long wedges

1 large orange (bell) pepper, halved,
    deseeded and cut into
    long wedges

2 fennel bulbs, cut into wedges

TAPENADE DRESSING

60 g/2½ oz. pitted
    black olives, drained

1 tablespoon capers, rinsed
    and patted dry

1 garlic clove, crushed

5 tablespoons extra virgin olive oil

large handful of flat leaf
    parsley leaves

sea salt and freshly ground
    black pepper

Serves 4

Vegetables take on a new dimension when roasted, becoming slightly sweet and smoky. The tapenade dressing adds to the Mediterranean feel of this salad, which can be served as a light meal or as an accompaniment to a larger dish.

Mix the olive oil and balsamic vinegar together in a large, shallow dish. Add the prepared vegetables, turn to coat them in the marinade, then leave to marinate while the oven is heating.

Preheat the oven to 200°C (400°F) Gas 6.

Turn out the vegetables into 2 large roasting pans and spread out into an even layer. Roast for 20 minutes, remove the courgettes/zucchini if tender, then return the rest of the vegetables to the oven and cook for a further 20 minutes, or until tender and blackened in places.

Meanwhile, to make the tapenade dressing, put the olives in a food processor or blender with the capers, garlic, olive oil and parsley, then pulse briefly until finely chopped and season to taste. Alternatively, coarsely chop all the ingredients by hand.

Serve the roasted vegetables warm or at room temperature, with some of the tapenade spooned over the top. (Transfer any remaining dressing to an airtight container and store in the refrigerator for up to 1 week.)

SHOOTS, FLOWERS & LEAVES

It's easy to forget to use flowers in food, but edible ones naturally lend themselves to salads, adding both colour and flavour. Here, courgette/zucchini, nasturtium and chive flowers are used, but feel free to experiment with others such as borage, marigolds, violas and pansies. Do make sure that the flowers have been grown organically and check that they are edible before use.

2 tablespoons extra virgin olive oil,
    plus extra for drizzling
1 yellow courgette/zucchini, sliced diagonally,
    plus flower, halved, if available
1 green courgette/zucchini, sliced diagonally,
    plus flower, halved, if available
100 g/3½ oz. rocket/arugula leaves
180 g/6 oz. char-grilled artichokes
handful of small nasturtium leaves
10 chive stems, snipped (with flowers if possible)
1 tablespoon lemon thyme leaves
freshly squeezed juice of ½ lemon
8 nasturtium flowers
sea salt and freshly ground black pepper

Serves 4

Heat the olive oil in a large frying pan/skillet over a medium heat and sauté the sliced courgettes/zucchini for 5 minutes, turning once, until tender and slightly golden. Leave to cool slightly.

Put the rocket/arugula on a serving plate and top with the courgettes/zucchini, artichokes, nasturtium leaves, snipped chives and lemon thyme. Squeeze over the lemon juice and drizzle with a little extra olive oil. Season and toss gently until combined.

Just before serving, garnish with the flowers.

JAPANESE WAKAME, RADISH & EDAMAME SALAD

Wakame is popular in miso soup, but this sea vegetable also makes a great addition to Japanese-style salads. It is mild and slightly sweet in taste, with a subtle saltiness reminiscent of the sea.

50 g/2 oz. frozen edamame beans
12 g/½ oz. dried wakame seaweed, rinsed
½ small cucumber, sliced into ribbons
115 g/4 oz. radishes, thinly sliced
    into rounds
70 g/3 oz. sugar snap peas,
    trimmed and sliced diagonally
2 spring onions/scallions,
    thinly sliced diagonally
2 teaspoons toasted sesame seeds

DRESSING
2 tablespoons sunflower oil
1 tablespoon sesame oil
2 tablespoons rice wine vinegar
1 tablespoon light soy sauce

Serves 4

Steam the edamame beans for 2–3 minutes until tender, then refresh under cold running water and drain.

Meanwhile, put the wakame in a bowl, pour over enough cold water to cover and leave to soak for 3 minutes until rehydrated, then drain.

Mix together all the ingredients for the dressing in a small bowl.

Put the cucumber in a large, shallow serving bowl with the cooked edamame beans, soaked wakame, radishes, sugar snap peas and spring onions/scallions. Spoon the dressing over and toss the salad until evenly coated. Sprinkle the sesame seeds over before serving.

SHREDDED CARROT & COURGETTE SALAD
WITH SESAME MISO SAUCE

2 carrots, grated
3 courgettes/zucchini, grated
30 g/¼ cup sesame seeds
150 g/1 cup firm tofu, chopped (optional)

MISO DRESSING
2 tablespoons miso paste
1 tablespoon rice wine vinegar
1 tablespoon sesame oil
2 tablespoons flaxseed oil
1 teaspoon finely sliced fresh ginger
2 teaspoons maple syrup

Serves 2–4

Vegetables take on a new personality when they are prepared differently.
The simple act of shredding veggies and mixing in a delicious dressing
is a tasty and beautiful way to treat our senses.

Put the carrots, courgettes/zucchini, sesame seeds and tofu (if using)
in a bowl.

For the dressing, whisk all of the ingredients together to an emulsion.
Pour over the mixed salad and serve.

The salad can be prepared in advance and stored in the refrigerator
for up to 2 days.

SPICY GREEN PAPAYA SALAD

1 young green papaya
2 carrots
1 garlic clove
1 Thai red chilli/chile (or jalapeño)
3 plum tomatoes, halved
220 g/1¾ cups green beans
90 g/¾ cup cashew nuts
a bunch of fresh coriander/cilantro
freshly squeezed juice of 2 limes
2 tablespoons soy sauce
1 tablespoon granulated stevia

Serves 2

Spicy food is often loaded with salt. If you're a spicy food addict try this
salad, which uses fresh chillies/chiles as a healthy way to get a spice fix.

Shred the green papaya and pat dry using paper towels. Transfer to a large
mixing bowl and grate in the carrots. Mix and set aside.

Crush the garlic and Thai red chilli/chile using a pestle and mortar (or you
can achieve the same effect by using the bottom of a rolling pin and a
chopping board). Add the tomatoes and the green beans and crush lightly
– you want the tomatoes to be bruised and the green beans to be soft.

Toast the cashew nuts in a dry frying pan/skillet set over a medium heat
until golden.

Put 60 g/½ cup of the toasted cashew nuts in a food processor and pulse
to a crumb. Transfer to the bowl with the papaya and carrot in. Add the
crushed tomato and green bean mixture, and the coriander/cilantro.

Add the lime juice, soy sauce and stevia and toss everything together.

Divide the salad between 2 serving dishes and top with the remaining
whole toasted cashews.

WILD RICE WITH ARTICHOKE, PEACHES & PINE NUTS

1 litre/4 cups water
190 g/1 cup wild rice
400 g/1½ cups artichokes soaked in water
    (rinsed and drained)
bunch of freshly chopped coriander/cilantro
30 g/¼ cup pine nuts
60 g/½ cup chopped peaches

DRESSING
3 tablespoons walnut oil
2 tablespoons freshly squeezed lemon juice
½ teaspoon sea salt
½ teaspoon freshly ground black pepper

Serves 2–4

Wild rice is actually an edible grass, which has a slightly nutty and chewy flavour. It forms the base of a great grain salad — just add your favourite veggies and a simple vinaigrette. Since it's a hearty grain, it is paired with soft artichokes, which are high in antioxidants.

Bring the water to a boil in a large saucepan or pot over a high heat. Add the wild rice, reduce the heat, cover and simmer for 45 minutes. Drain any excess water and set aside.

For the dressing, whisk together the walnut oil, lemon juice, salt and pepper in a large bowl.

Then once the rice has cooled a bit but is still slightly warm, mix in the dressing with the artichokes, half of the coriander/cilantro, the pine nuts and peaches.

Serve garnished with the rest of the coriander/cilantro.

KIMCHI, AVOCADO & ALFALFA SALAD

2 Chinese leaves/Chinese cabbage,
    shredded
2 spring onions/scallions, shredded
1 red chilli/chile, deseeded and diced
2.5-cm/1-in. piece fresh root ginger,
    peeled and very thinly sliced
2 tablespoons black sesame seeds, toasted
4 tablespoons rice vinegar
4 teaspoons caster/superfine sugar
½ teaspoon sea salt
75 g/3 oz. baby spinach leaves
2 avocados, halved, stoned/pitted,
    peeled and sliced
2 tablespoons cold-pressed rapeseed oil
2 handfuls of alfalfa sprouts

Serves 4

Kimchi, the highly popular Korean pickle, traditionally takes a few days to make and ferment, but with this 'cheat's' version, it needs a comparatively short amount of time, just enough to let the flavours meld and mingle.

First make the kimchi. Mix together the Chinese leaves/Chinese cabbage, spring onions/scallions, chilli/chile, ginger, sesame seeds, rice vinegar, caster/superfine sugar and salt in a bowl and leave to sit for 30 minutes (or longer if time allows) to let the flavours develop.

Just before serving, divide the spinach and avocados between four serving plates, drizzle with the oil and top with the kimchi and alfalfa sprouts.

CHAR-GRILLED ASPARAGUS WITH HERB OIL

300 g/11 oz. asparagus spears,
 ends trimmed

HERB OIL
3 tablespoons extra virgin olive oil,
 plus extra for brushing
large handful of mixed finely chopped
 herbs, such as basil, oregano and thyme
1 small garlic clove, crushed
freshly squeezed juice of ½ lemon
sea salt and freshly ground black pepper

Serves 4

Make the most of the short asparagus season with this deliciously simple and easy salad. The slightly charred spears are drizzled with a light, fragrant herb oil instead of the more usual mayonnaise or hollandaise sauce.

To make the herb oil, mix together all the ingredients in a bowl and season to taste. Set aside while you griddle the asparagus.

Heat a large, ridged griddle pan over a high heat. Brush the asparagus spears with oil and season. Griddle the asparagus, in two batches, for 5–8 minutes, turning them occasionally, or until tender and slightly charred in places. Serve the asparagus drizzled with the herb oil.

LONG-STEM BROCCOLI WITH LEMON-MUSTARD DRESSING

400 g/14 oz. long-stem broccoli, trimmed
small handful of radish sprouts (optional)

LEMON-MUSTARD DRESSING
3 tablespoons extra virgin olive oil
1 garlic clove, finely chopped
2 tablespoons freshly squeezed lemon juice
1 teaspoon Dijon mustard
sea salt and freshly ground black pepper

Serves 4

The lemon-mustard dressing enlivens the stems of lightly steamed broccoli in this easy side salad. If you can't find long-stem broccoli, use regular broccoli instead.

Steam the broccoli for 2–3 minutes until only just tender, then refresh under cold running water to prevent it cooking any further and to keep its colour. Drain.

Meanwhile, make the dressing. Heat the oil and garlic in a small pan over a low heat for 1 minute, then stir in the lemon juice and mustard, season and warm through briefly.

Arrange the broccoli on a serving plate, spoon the dressing over and sprinkle the radish sprouts on top, if using.

MID-WEEK
SUPPERS

HEALING AZUKI BEAN STEW WITH AMARANTH

This stew is made with only a couple of ingredients, the consistency is rich and creamy and the taste slightly sweet. After travelling or a stressful day, this stew will take all your worries away!

200 g/1 cup dried azuki beans
1 litre/4 cups cold water
180 g/1½ cups peeled, deseeded and cubed Hokkaido or kabocha pumpkin
70 g/⅓ cup amaranth
2 tablespoons soy sauce
½ tablespoon umeboshi vinegar
½ teaspoon ground turmeric
½ teaspoon sea salt

Serves 2–3

Cover the azuki beans with the water in a saucepan and soak overnight (this is not necessary but will speed up the cooking). Bring them to a boil in the soaking water, then add the pumpkin and cook, half-covered, over a low heat until the azuki are half-done (about 30 minutes). Add the amaranth and cook until both the azuki and amaranth are soft (another 20–30 minutes). Season with the remaining ingredients and adjust the thickness by adding hot water, if necessary.

This stew doesn't have any oil and provides the body with a lot of well-balanced nutrients. It is a great winter dish when you feel exhausted and need comfort food that is easy to digest.

MIXED VEGETABLE PLATTER

You can use pretty much any combination of vegetables that you like for this platter, but remember to cook them separately, as it's best not to crowd the barbecue/grill.

1 aubergine/eggplant, cut into 5-mm/¼-in. thick slices
4 field mushrooms
bunch of thin asparagus spears
1 celery stick, cut into 3-cm/1¼-in. lengths
1 red (bell) pepper, cut into 2-cm/¾-in. wide strips
vegetable oil, for brushing
steamed rice, to serve (optional)

SOY BALSAMIC MARINADE
125 ml/½ cup light soy sauce
65 ml/¼ cup balsamic vinegar
1 tablespoon olive oil
2 teaspoons white sugar

Serves 4

Put all of the ingredients for the marinade in a small bowl and whisk to combine. Arrange the vegetables in a large, non-metallic flat dish and pour over the marinade. Use your hands to toss the vegetables around in the marinade until evenly coated. Cover and let sit for 1 hour, turning often, to allow the flavours to develop.

Preheat the barbecue, hotplate or grill to high and brush lightly with vegetable oil. Use tongs to transfer the vegetables to a plate and reserve the marinade. Cook the aubergine/eggplant and mushrooms first, for 2–3 minutes on each side, until dark brown, basting once or twice with a little of the reserved marinade. Transfer to a warmed serving plate. Put the asparagus, celery and red (bell) pepper on the barbecue and cook for 3–4 minutes on each side, basting with a little of the marinade as necessary. Transfer the vegetables to the serving plate with the aubergine/eggplant and mushrooms.

Serve with steamed rice, if liked. Any remaining marinade can be poured into a jug/pitcher and used as a sauce.

RICE NOODLE & SMOKED TOFU BOWL

The ingredients for this Asian main meal salad may look on the long side, but it's very easy to prepare and can be made the night before and packed the next day for lunch. If making in advance, assemble the salad just before serving.

2 tablespoons coconut oil
or sunflower oil
275 g/10 oz. smoked tofu, drained,
patted dry and cut into
bite-sized cubes
200 g/7 oz. dried rice vermicelli
noodles
1 carrot, halved crossways and
thinly sliced into thin strips
10-cm/4-in. piece cucumber,
quartered lengthways, seeded
and thinly sliced into strips
2 handfuls of shredded sweetheart/
pointed cabbage
3 spring onions/scallions,
thinly sliced
½ red onion, thinly sliced
2 handfuls of freshly chopped
mint leaves
2 handfuls of freshly torn basil leaves
1 Little Gem/Bibb lettuce,
leaves separated
75 g/⅓ cup salted peanuts,
roughly chopped

DRESSING
5 tablespoons rice wine vinegar
4 teaspoons caster/superfine sugar
1 tablespoon vegan fish sauce
(see page 18)
1 red chilli/chile, seeded and diced

Serves 4

Heat the oil in a large frying pan/skillet over a medium heat and fry the tofu for 8–10 minutes, turning often, until golden and crisp. Drain on paper towels.

Meanwhile, prepare the noodles as instructed on the packet, then drain and refresh under cold running water and drain again. Transfer the noodles to a large bowl. Mix together all the ingredients for the dressing and pour over the noodles.

Add the carrot, cucumber, cabbage, spring onions/scallions, red onion and half the herbs to the noodles and toss until combined. Arrange the Little Gem/Bibb leaves on a large, flat serving plate and top with the noodle salad, smoked tofu, remaining herbs and peanuts.

Smoked tofu
The beauty of smoked tofu is that it doesn't need to be marinated before use. Try to find a brand that naturally smokes the tofu, rather than pump it with a smoke flavouring. Tofu is sold packed in water, so must be drained well and patted dry with paper towels before frying, otherwise you may have difficulty in getting it to crisp up.

STICKY SESAME AUBERGINE WITH GOCHUJANG KETCHUP

2 aubergines/eggplants

2 tablespoons sesame oil

2 tablespoons olive oil

4-cm/1½-in. piece of fresh root ginger,
  peeled and grated

4 tablespoons ketjap manis
  (thick, sweet Indonesian soy sauce)

120 ml/½ cup dark soy sauce

4 teaspoons gochujang paste

2 teaspoons caster/granulated sugar

3 garlic cloves, chopped

2–3 tablespoons sesame seeds

bunch of spring onions/scallions, chopped

4 pitta breads, warmed, to serve

shredded lettuce, to serve

FOR THE GOCHUJANG KETCHUP

4 tablespoons gochujang paste

4 tablespoons good-quality tomato ketchup

Serves 4

Gochujang paste is an easy marinade for chunks of aubergine/eggplant, which absorb the glorious flavours and transform into toothsome loveliness.

Preheat the oven to 190°C (375°F) Gas 5. Cut the aubergines/eggplants into bite-sized cubes and transfer them to a large bowl. In a separate bowl, mix the sesame oil, olive oil, grated ginger, ketjap manis, soy sauce, 4 teaspoons gochujang paste, sugar and garlic. Stir everything together and pour the mixture over the aubergine/eggplant cubes. Toss to coat everything well. Spoon the aubergine/eggplant evenly over a large, flat baking sheet and roast for about 25–30 minutes, until the aubergine/eggplant is cooked. Scatter over the sesame seeds and chopped spring onions/scallions.

To make the gochujang ketchup, simply mix the 4 tablespoons gochujang paste with the tomato ketchup in a small bowl.

Scoop the aubergine/eggplant mixture into warmed pitta breads, and add shredded lettuce and gochujang ketchup, as desired.

RATATOUILLE BAKED BEANS

1 aubergine/eggplant,
  cut into 2-cm/¾-in. cubes

1 red (bell) pepper, deseeded and
  cut into 2-cm/¾-in. pieces

¼ large butternut squash, deseeded,
  peeled and cut into 2-cm/¾-in. cubes

1 onion, cut into 8 wedges

1 tablespoon olive oil

1 teaspoon sea salt

400-g/14-oz. can cannellini beans,
  drained and rinsed

12 stoned/pitted black olives, halved

400-g/14-oz. can chopped tomatoes

2 tablespoons tomato purée/paste

1 teaspoon maple syrup

1½ teaspoons freshly chopped basil leaves

Serves 4

A combination of two classics – ratatouille and baked beans – this dish is delightfully flavoursome. This is an ideal mid-week vegan meal to enjoy with friends or family.

Preheat the oven to 200°C (400°F) Gas 6.

Place the chopped aubergine/eggplant, (bell) pepper, squash and onion on a baking pan with sides.

Drizzle over the olive oil and sprinkle over the salt. Bake in the preheated oven for 30 minutes until the vegetables are soft.

Add the cannellini beans, black olives, chopped tomatoes, tomato purée/paste and maple syrup and stir. Bake for a further 10 minutes. Serve with the basil scattered over the top.

Serve with crushed new potatoes.

QUINOA BURGERS WITH PORTOBELLO MUSHROOMS

This is your new go-to vegan burger! Quinoa is moist and mixes with sweet potato and black beans to give a meaty consistency.

3 tablespoons olive oil
1 onion, finely chopped
2 garlic cloves, crushed
75 g/¹/₂ cup black beans
120 g/²/₃ cup cooked quinoa
    (see Note)
100 g/¹/₂ cup sweet potato,
    flesh scooped out
1 carrot, shredded
¹/₂ teaspoon ground cumin
¹/₂ teaspoon ground coriander
2 tablespoons parsley, chopped
15 g/¹/₈ cup breadcrumbs
5 portobello mushrooms
sea salt and freshly ground
    black pepper

TO SERVE
1 avocado, stone/pitted, peeled
    and sliced
1 large tomato, sliced
1 gherkin/pickle, chopped
¹/₂ red onion, sliced
handful of fresh coriander/cilantro
1–2 tablespoons freshly squeezed
    lime juice
baking sheet, lined with
    baking parchment

Makes 5 burgers

Preheat the oven to 180°C (350°F) Gas 4.

Heat 1 tablespoon of the olive oil in a saucepan or pot over a medium heat. Fry the onion for about 3 minutes, until softened. Add the garlic and cook for another minute. Then add the beans, stir and cook for a few minutes longer. Remove from the heat and transfer the mixture to a large mixing bowl.

Lightly mash the beans with a fork until they're semi-crushed. Add the rest of the ingredients (except the mushrooms and remaining olive oil) to the bowl, add salt and pepper and mix well. If the mixture is too moist, add extra breadcrumbs. If too dry, add some more smashed beans.

Form patties with your hands and place on the prepared baking sheet. Bake in the preheated oven for 20–25 minutes, checking after about 15 minutes and turning once to insure even browning. Once cooked remove from the main oven and keep warm in a cool oven or hot plate.

Increase the temperature of the oven to 200°C (400°F) Gas 6.

For the mushroom base, clean the mushrooms with a damp cloth. Remove the stems and drizzle with the remaining 2 tablespoons olive oil. Season with salt and pepper and roast for 20 minutes.

When ready to serve, place each burger on top of a roasted mushroom and garnish with your choice of burger toppings.

Note To prepare a basic cooked quinoa, put 210 g/1¹/₄ cups quinoa in a frying pan/skillet with 240 ml/1 cup stock and 200 ml/³/₄ cup water. Bring to the boil then reduce the temperature. Cover and simmer for 20 minutes. Uncover, fluff with a fork and set aside for 5 minutes before using.

30 g/³/₄ cup coconut chips
3 tablespoons vegetable oil
1 large cauliflower, finely chopped
1 lemongrass stalk, tough outer layers
    removed, finely chopped
4 fresh kaffir lime leaves, thinly sliced
3 green Thai chillies/chiles, finely chopped
4 tablespoons soy sauce
freshly squeezed juice of 1 lime
5 spring onions/scallions, thinly sliced
10 g/¹/₂ cup coriander/cilantro, leaves
    picked and chopped
10 g/¹/₂ cup mint, leaves picked
    and chopped
sea salt

TO SERVE
lettuce leaves
cooked jasmine rice
purple basil (optional)

Serves 4

CAULIFLOWER LARB
WITH COCONUT RICE & FRESH LEAVES

Larb is a flavoursome dish from Northern Thailand that is usually made
with meat and served as a salad with rice and crisp leaves.

Heat a wok or a large, heavy-based frying pan/skillet over a medium-high heat.
Add the coconut chips and cook, stirring, for 2 minutes or until golden brown.
Remove from the heat. Transfer to the bowl of a food processor and process
until finely ground. Set aside.

Heat the oil in the wok or frying pan/skillet over a high heat. Add the cauliflower,
lemongrass, kaffir lime leaves, chillies/chiles, soy sauce and lime juice and cook,
stirring occasionally, for 5 minutes or until the cauliflower changes colour.
Transfer to a heatproof bowl and set aside for 15 minutes to cool.

Toss the spring onions/scallions, coriander/cilantro and mint into the cauliflower
mixture. Season with salt. Serve with lettuce leaves and cooked jasmine rice
mixed with the finely ground toasted coconut. Garnish with purple basil, if you like.

2 baking potatoes
10 artichoke heart quarters, preserved in oil
about 20 olives (black or green), preserved
    in olive oil or marinated if you prefer
large handful of rocket/arugula

CAPER PARSLEY DRESSING
grated zest and freshly squeezed juice
    of 1 lemon
1 tablespoon olive oil
2 teaspoons Dijon mustard
1 tablespoon freshly chopped parsley
2 teaspoons baby capers
sea salt and freshly ground black pepper

Serves 2

BAKED POTATO WITH ARTICHOKE & OLIVE
ROCKET SALAD WITH PARSLEY CAPER DRESSING

Baked here with artichokes, olives form a fresh and delicious warm salad
filling for a jacket potato finished with a tangy lemon and caper dressing.

Preheat the oven to 200°C (400°F) Gas 6. Prick the skin of the potato.
Bake in the preheated oven for about 50 minutes–1 hour. Reduce the oven
temperature to 180°C (350°F) Gas 4. Place the artichokes and olives on a
baking sheet and bake in the preheated oven for about 5–10 minutes.

Prepare the dressing by whisking together the lemon zest and juice, olive oil
and mustard until emulsified. Whisk in the parsley and capers. If you can only
get large capers rather than baby capers, roughly chop them with a sharp
knife. Season the dressing with salt and pepper.

To serve, cut each potato open. Toss the rocket/arugula with the artichokes
and olives (together with any roasting juices) and divide between the
potatoes. Drizzle the dressing over the potatoes. Serve straight away.

OODLES OF ZOODLES

'Zoodles' or courgette/zucchini noodles, are gaining in popularity as an alternative to traditional pastas. They look exactly like spaghetti and can be used in the same way to provide an everyday spaghetti-lite. These are delicious served with a simple vegan red or green pesto.

2 courgettes/zucchini, trimmed
sea salt and freshly ground
    black pepper
a handful of fresh basil, to serve

RED PESTO
60 g/tightly packed ½ cup sun-dried
    tomatoes in oil, drained
125 g/1 cup pine nuts
1 roasted garlic clove
3–4 tablespoons olive oil
½ teaspoon dried basil
¼ teaspoon dried oregano

MACADAMIA 'PARMESAN'
60 g/½ cup macadamia nuts
4 tablespoons nutritional yeast
¼ teaspoon salt

spiralizer

Serves 4

Begin by preparing the zoodles. Slice the courgettes/zucchini using a spiralizer and set aside until you are ready to serve.

To make the red pesto, put all of the ingredients in a food processor with a little black pepper and pulse until smooth, adding more olive oil to loosen the mixture if necessary. Transfer to a bowl and set aside.

Rinse the food processor and pulse all of the macadamia 'Parmesan' ingredients together to a fine crumb.

When you are ready to serve, bring a saucepan or pot of water to the boil over a medium–high heat. Add the zoodles and cook for 2 minutes, taking care not to let them overcook. Drain in a fine mesh sieve/strainer and return the zoodles to the pan. Add 1 tablespoon of the red pesto to the pan and set over a gentle heat for 1 minute to warm the pesto.

Warm the remaining red pesto in a separate saucepan or pot set over a gentle heat for 2–3 minutes.

Divide the mixture between two bowls, top with the warm red pesto and sprinkle over the macadamia 'Parmesan'. Garnish each with a few fresh basil leaves and serve.

ROASTED SUMMER VEGETABLES

1 red onion, halved and finely sliced
4 mushrooms, thinly sliced
10 cherry tomatoes, halved
½ courgette/zucchini, thinly sliced
   using a mandoline
2 teaspoons olive oil
½ teaspoon sea salt
freshly squeezed juice of ¼ lemon
1 tablespoon fresh basil leaves

Serves 2

A Mediterranean mix of vegetables and flavours. This dish would be complemented by some avocado slices with lemon juice and black pepper and some hummus.

Preheat the oven to 200°C (400°F) Gas 6.

Put all of the vegetables on a sheet pan with sides. Drizzle over the olive oil, then sprinkle over the salt.

Bake in the preheated oven for 20 minutes. Stir once during baking.

When you are ready to serve, squeeze over the lemon juice and sprinkle over the basil leaves. Serve with avocado slices, hummus and lemon wedges.

POTATO & ROSEMARY PIZZA

PIZZA BASE
500 g/3½–3⅔ cups strong bread flour
1 teaspoon fine sea salt
1 teaspoon caster/granulated sugar
7-g/¼-oz. sachet fast-action dried yeast
1 tablespoon olive oil
about 300 ml/1¼ cups hand-hot water

TOPPING
600 g/21 oz. smallish floury potatoes,
   soaked and very thinly sliced
4 tablespoons olive oil
2 tablespoons finely chopped rosemary
large bunch of spring onions/scallions,
   chopped
sea salt and freshly ground black pepper

Serves 4

This pizza is made from the kind of staples you generally have in the house – and if you use fast-action yeast, it doesn't take too long from start to finish either. Simplicity at its winning best.

Preheat the oven to 200°C (400°F) Gas 6. Put the flour into a large bowl and stir in the salt and sugar. Add the yeast and mix well. Pour in the olive oil, and add enough hand-hot water to bring the mixture together into a soft, but not sticky dough. Knead the dough for 5–10 minutes, until smooth.

Divide the dough into two and roll each piece into a rectangle to fit the base of two sheet pans.

Drain the water from the potatoes and rinse them under running cold water. Dry thoroughly on paper towels or a clean kitchen towel. Toss them into a large bowl with the olive oil, rosemary and a generous sprinkling of salt and black pepper, until all the slices are evenly coated.

Scatter the spring onions/scallions between the two bases. Top with the potato slices, overlapping the potato edges very slightly, until the bases are covered. Bake the pizzas for about 20 minutes or so, until the potatoes are cooked and crispy golden at the edges. Cut into squares and serve at once.

5 tablespoons frozen peas

2 large handfuls frozen
butternut squash pieces

2 handfuls frozen spinach

300 ml/1¼ cups coconut milk

1 teaspoon freshly squeezed lime
or lemon juice

2½ teaspoons tamari or soy sauce

1 teaspoon coconut sugar

1½ teaspoons dried Thai spice mix

freshly chopped coriander/cilantro
or Thai basil leaves, to garnish

Serves 4

SIMPLE THAI VEGETABLES

Thai flavours are so aromatic and exotic-tasting. This is a great dish to make when you're caught short and have very little fresh food in.

Preheat the oven to 200°C (400°F) Gas 6.

Put the frozen peas, butternut squash and spinach in a deep-sided sheet pan.

Put the coconut milk, lime or lemon juice, tamari or soy sauce, coconut sugar and Thai spice mix in a bowl and mix together. Pour the mixture over the vegetables and stir.

Bake in the preheated oven for 30 minutes, stirring twice during baking.

Garnish with the fresh herbs and serve hot with rice.

2 tablespoons coconut oil

2 tablespoons green curry paste (check
the label says it is vegan, if needed)

1 red onion, sliced

4 garlic cloves, crushed

200 g/7 oz. tenderstem cauliflower
or cauliflower florets

1 red (bell) pepper, deseeded
and thinly sliced

2 purple or normal carrots, peeled
and sliced diagonally

2 baby pak choi/bok choy, halved

100 g/3½ oz. mangetout/snow peas

1 tablespoon palm sugar/jaggery

1 tablespoon liquid aminos (or tamari)

400 g/14 oz. can coconut milk

3 kaffir lime leaves

freshly squeezed juice of 1 lime

sea salt and freshly ground black pepper

TO SERVE
bunch of purple Thai basil
sambal oelek (optional)
cooked rice
lime wedges

Serves 4

THAI GREEN CAULI CURRY

Aromatic, creamy, fresh and zingy, just like a good Thai curry should be. The addition of liquid aminos in place of the traditional fish sauce adds a depth of flavour and extra umami goodness.

In a large pan or wok set over a medium-high heat, heat 1 tablespoon of the coconut oil, being cautious of it spitting.

Add the curry paste and fry it, stirring it into the coconut oil, for about 1 minute. Turn the heat down, add the onion and cook until the onion is slightly translucent, about 8 minutes.

Add the garlic, stir together, then add the second tablespoon of coconut oil. Add the cauliflower, red (bell) pepper, carrots, pak choi/bok choy and mangetout/snow peas. Add the palm sugar/jaggery, liquid aminos (or tamari) and some salt and pepper and stir everything together. Reduce the heat to medium and cook down, stirring, until the carrots are tender-crisp, about 10–15 minutes.

Add the coconut milk and kaffir lime leaves, stir, and then let it simmer for about 5 minutes. Squeeze the lime juice over, stir, and then remove from the heat.

Add the purple Thai basil and stir in the sambal oelek, if using. Serve with rice and lime wedges.

QUICK CAULIFLOWER RICE SAFFRON PILAF

50 ml/3½ tablespoons coconut cream
large pinch of saffron threads
1 head of cauliflower, core removed
   and cut into florets
1 tablespoon coconut oil
1 onion, finely chopped
1 tablespoon pomegranate seeds
1 tablespoon pistachios
sea salt and freshly ground black pepper
micro herbs, to garnish (optional)

Serves 2

This is the perfect low-carb dish. For a quick, healthy meal, serve this with lots of steamed green vegetables and some chilli sauce.

Warm the coconut cream through in a small saucepan over a low heat. Turn off the heat, then add the saffron threads and leave to steep.

In 2–3 batches, add the cauliflower florets to a food processor with the blade attachment and pulse a few times until processed into rice-sized pieces.

Add the coconut oil to a medium sauté pan over a medium heat. When the oil is hot, add the onion and sauté for about 3–4 minutes or until translucent.

Add the cauliflower 'rice' and sauté for 10 minutes until slightly browned. Turn the heat down to low, then stir in the coconut saffron mixture and allow to absorb for a few minutes. Finally, stir through the pomegranate seeds and pistachios and season. Serve garnished with micro herbs, if you like.

AUBERGINE, TOMATO & RED LENTIL CURRY

3 tablespoons light olive oil
1 large aubergine/eggplant,
   cut into 8 pieces
1 red onion, chopped
2 garlic cloves, chopped
1 tablespoon finely chopped fresh ginger
250 g/9 oz. cherry tomatoes on the vine
6–8 curry leaves
1 teaspoon ground cumin
¼ teaspoon chilli/chili powder
1 tablespoon tomato purée/paste
125 g/4½ oz. red split lentils
handful of freshly chopped
   coriander/cilantro
boiled or steamed basmati rice,
   to serve (optional)

Serves 4

So many iconic international meat-free dishes are based on aubergine, it works so well with a host Asian and Mediterranean flavours.

Heat the oil in a frying pan/skillet set over a high heat. When the oil is smoking hot add the aubergine/eggplant to the pan and cook for 5 minutes, turning the pieces often so that they cook evenly. At first the aubergine/eggplant will absorb the oil, but as it cooks to a dark and golden colour, the oil will start to seep out back into the pan. Remove from the pan at this point and not before.

Add the onions, garlic and ginger to the pan and cook for 5 minutes. Add the cherry tomatoes and cook for 1 minute, until they just soften and collapse, then remove them from the pan before they break up too much and set aside with the aubergine/eggplant.

Add the curry leaves and cumin to the pan and cook for a couple of minutes as the curry leaves pop and crackle. Add the chilli powder, tomato purée, 480 ml/ 2 cups water and the lentils and simmer for 15–20 minutes, until the lentils are tender but retain some 'bite'. Stir in the aubergine/eggplant and cherry tomatoes and cook the curry for a couple of minutes just to warm through. Stir in the coriander/cilantro and spoon over basmati rice to serve, if liked.

5 shallots, very finely chopped

2 small garlic cloves, very finely chopped

2-cm/¾-in. piece of fresh root ginger, peeled and grated

2 teaspoons ground cumin

¾ teaspoon ground coriander

1 teaspoon ground turmeric

400-g/14-oz. can tomatoes

400-g/14-oz. can coconut milk

½ yellow (bell) pepper, deseeded and thinly sliced

½ red (bell) pepper, deseeded and thinly sliced

½ orange (bell) pepper, deseeded and thinly sliced

2 x 400-g/14-oz. cans chickpeas, drained and rinsed

freshly chopped coriander/cilantro, to serve

Serves 4

1 onion, sliced

2 garlic cloves, chopped

4 tablespoons olive oil

2 tablespoons Berbere spice mix

2 large carrots

1 large sweet potato (about 250 g/9 oz.), peeled and cut into bite-sized chunks

400-g/14-oz. can chopped tomatoes

4-cm/1½-in. piece of fresh root ginger, grated

450 ml/scant 2 cups passata/strained tomatoes

800 ml/generous 3¼ cups well-flavoured vegetable stock

2 tablespoons good-quality tomato ketchup

150 g/scant 1 cup dried red lentils, rinsed

large handful of fresh baby spinach leaves

bunch of freshly chopped parsley

chilli/chile oil, to serve (optional)

Serves 4

CHICKPEA & PEPPER CURRY BAKE

Chickpeas and (bell) peppers combine beautifully in this dish to bring sweetness, tanginess and yet the mellowness of a substantial vegan baked meal-in-one.

Preheat the oven to 220°C (425°F) Gas 7.

Mix the shallots, garlic, ginger, spices, tomatoes and coconut milk together in a bowl or food processor.

Put the sliced (bell) peppers on a sheet pan with sides. Pour over the coconut milk and spice mixture. Cover with foil and bake in the preheated oven for 30 minutes.

Add the chickpeas to the curry mix and stir. Bake for another 5 minutes. Sprinkle over the coriander/cilantro and serve with rice.

ETHIOPIAN LENTIL CASSEROLE

This Ethiopian-influenced lentil stew is great when you're craving something fuss-free and filling but full on flavour.

Preheat the oven to 190°C (375°F) Gas 5. Scatter the onion over the base of a deep roasting pan. Add the garlic to the pan, drizzle everything with the olive oil and scatter over the berbere spice mix. Give it a good stir to coat everything in the spice mix and cook for 10 minutes.

Cut the carrots into triangular-shaped chunks. Remove the roasting pan from the oven and toss in the carrots and sweet potato. Pour in the chopped tomatoes and stir in the grated ginger. Add the passata/strained tomatoes, stock and tomato ketchup. Stir in the lentils, cover with foil and cook for 30–35 minutes, until the vegetables and lentils are soft and the casserole is nicely thickened.

Stir in the spinach leaves and half of the parsley, and return the pan to the oven for a further 3–4 minutes. Serve with an extra scattering of chopped parsley, and chilli/chile oil, if desired.

FEEDING
A CROWD

WILD MUSHROOM & LEEK RISOTTO

900 ml/3¾ cups vegetable
  stock/broth (make your own by
  covering carrots, onion, celery,
  bay leaf, parsley, thyme and
  a few peppercorns with water
  and simmering for ½ hour)
extra virgin olive oil
1 large onion, finely chopped
2 leeks, chopped
6 garlic cloves, finely chopped
350 g/1¾ cups Arborio or
  Carnaroli rice
glass of dry white wine
200 ml/¾ cup soy cream/creamer
300 g/10 oz. mixed wild mushrooms
3 tablespoons finely chopped parsley
sea salt and freshly ground
  black pepper

Serves 6–8

It's nice to think that a dish you associate with butter, cream and Parmesan can be just as enjoyable and indulgent when made with vegan alternatives. Soy cream/creamer gives it that velvety smoothness. It has the same consistency as normal cream, and the slight difference in taste is undetectable in the risotto when seasoned properly.

Bring and keep the vegetable stock/broth in a saucepan just under boiling point, ready to add into the risotto.

Heat 3 tablespoons oil in a heavy-based pan, add the onion and leeks and cook gently over a low heat until they are completely soft and translucent. You do not want to colour them. Add 5 of the chopped garlic cloves, turn up the heat and stir for 1 minute. Add the rice, stirring frequently until the grains are completely covered in oil and beginning to turn translucent.

Pour in the glass of wine (it should steam and bubble) and season with a pinch of salt. Gradually add the hot stock a ladleful at a time, adding another ladle each time the liquid has been absorbed by the rice.

When the stock is finished, stir through the soy cream/creamer and some pepper. Season to taste, then turn down the heat.

In a separate pan, warm a little oil over a medium-high heat. Add the mushrooms and fry for 1–2 minutes until the mushrooms have softened and coloured a little.

Add the mushrooms to the risotto. Make a quick parsley oil by combining the chopped parsley with the remaining chopped garlic clove and as much oil as you like. Drizzle over the risotto and serve immediately.

ULTIMATE VEGGIE ROAST

1 red onion, roughly chopped
200 g/7 oz. mixed peeled butternut squash
    flesh and sweet potato, diced
200 g/7 oz. chestnut mushrooms, chopped
1 red (bell) pepper, deseeded and diced
6 garlic cloves, unpeeled
4 tablespoons olive oil, plus extra for brushing
400-g/14-oz. can butter/lima beans,
    drained and rinsed
250 g/9 oz. mixed nuts, toasted
30 g/1 oz. dried porcini mushrooms,
    soaked and drained
3 fresh rosemary sprigs, leaves picked
bunch of fresh thyme, leaves picked,
    reserving some to garnish
bunch of fresh parsley, leaves picked
100 g/3½ oz. pitted green olives,
    roughly chopped
4 spring onions/scallions, finely chopped
50 g/⅓ cup mixed raisins
20 g/2 tablespoons capers, drained (optional)
2 tablespoons soy sauce
60 g/generous 1 cup fresh breadcrumbs
freshly squeezed juice of ½ lemon
sea salt and freshly ground black pepper
pomegranate seeds, fresh sage leaves and
    purple basil, to garnish (optional)

TO LINE THE PAN

1 large or 2 small aubergine/eggplants,
    thinly sliced lengthways
2–3 courgettes/zucchini, thinly sliced
    lengthways

griddle pan/grill pan

*20-cm/8-in, deep springform baking pan,
lightly greased with oil and base-lined
with baking parchment*

Serves 4–6

This show-stopping roast contains many delicious layers of flavour. It can also be a great recipe to feed a family for a few days – a lot of goodness packed into one meal!

Preheat the oven to 200°C (400°F) Gas 6.

Toss the onion, butternut squash, sweet potato, chestnut mushrooms and red (bell) pepper with the garlic and 2 tablespoons of the oil in a large bowl. Spread out in a large roasting pan and roast in the preheated oven for 25–30 minutes, until soft, turning once.

Meanwhile, prepare the pan lining. Preheat the griddle pan/grill pan over a medium-high heat. Brush the aubergine/eggplant and courgette/zucchini slices with the remaining oil and season with salt and pepper. Griddle for 1–2 minutes on each side until lightly charred, then set aside to cool until needed.

Add the roasted vegetables and garlic to a food processor and pulse to a chunky purée. Set aside in a large mixing bowl.

Place the butter/lima beans, nuts, re-hydrated porcini mushrooms and herbs in the food processor and pulse to roughly chop. Add to the bowl with the roasted vegetable purée along with the olives, spring onions/scallions, raisins, capers (if using), soy sauce, breadcrumbs and lemon juice. Season with salt and pepper and mix together until well combined.

Preheat the oven to 160°C (325°F) Gas 3.

Line the base of the prepared baking pan with alternating slices of courgette/zucchini and aubergine/eggplant, overlapping slightly, until the base and sides are totally covered. Pile the vegetable filling in and pack down gently. Place the remaining grilled vegetable slices over the top to completely cover the filling, tucking in or trimming untidy edges. Brush with oil and scatter with the reserved thyme. Cover the pan with foil and roast in the preheated oven for 40 minutes, uncovering 10 minutes before the end of the cooking time until the top turns golden.

Rest for 5 minutes in the pan, then loosen the edges with a knife and carefully turn out onto a serving plate. Garnish with pomegranate seeds, sage and purple basil leaves, if liked, before serving.

BUTTERNUT SQUASH FALAFELS
WITH FIG, CHIOGGIA BEETROOT & CHILLI OIL

Chickpea falafel can be a little tricky to make, but this butternut squash variety is really simple. You could use any kind of squash really, or sweet potato works well too. Here, they are paired with juicy figs, chioggia beetroot/beet, some bitter radicchio leaves and spicy oil.

1 chioggia beetroot/beet,
    very thinly sliced
radicchio leaves
handful of lamb's lettuce
    or rocket/arugula
grated zest and freshly squeezed
    juice of 1 lemon
4 fresh figs
1 fresh red chilli/chile, deseeded
    and finely chopped
extra virgin olive oil
sea salt
balsamic vinegar

FALAFEL

1 butternut squash, peeled,
    deseeded and cut into chunks
1 teaspoon each cumin and coriander
    seeds, gently toasted in a dry
    pan until fragrant
1 teaspoon ground cinnamon
2 garlic cloves
3 tablespoons freshly chopped
    coriander/cilantro
squeeze of lemon juice
4–6 tablespoons gram flour
extra virgin olive oil
sea salt

Serves 4–6

Preheat the oven to 200°C (400°F) Gas 6.

To make the falafel, toss the butternut squash with some oil and salt on a baking sheet. Roast in the preheated oven for about 30 minutes or until the squash takes on a little colour and is cooked through.

Meanwhile, using a pestle and mortar, pound the cumin and coriander seeds until finely ground. Add the cinnamon, garlic and a good pinch of salt and pound again to a paste.

When the squash is cooked, remove from the oven and allow to cool slightly. Leave the oven on.

Put the squash in a mixing bowl and mash with a fork. Transfer to a sieve/strainer to drain for a few minutes, then lightly press with a spoon to drain off any remaining water. Put back in the bowl, add the spice paste, the coriander/cilantro and lemon juice and mix together. Add the gram flour a tablespoon at a time until the mixture is still quite loose and sticky but holds its shape when scooped out. Using 2 teaspoons, spoon the mixture onto a baking sheet, shaping with your fingers to create falafel shapes.

Roast in the oven for about 15–20 minutes, until they take on a bit of colour and firm up.

When the falafels are ready, season the beetroot/beet, radicchio and lamb's lettuce with the lemon zest and juice, some olive oil and salt.

To serve, arrange the falafel and dressed salad on individual plates or a large serving dish. Tear open the figs and drizzle a little vinegar onto their flesh and around the plate. Combine the chopped chilli/chile with some olive oil and drizzle over. Serve immediately.

80 g/½ cup couscous
125 ml/½ cup boiling water
200 g/1 cup leftover chickpea-based
    hummus
50 g/¼ cup finely grated vegetables
    (beetroots/beets, carrots, parsnip,
    celeriac/celery root, etc.)
40 g/1 small onion, finely chopped
2 garlic cloves, finely chopped
½ teaspoon dried oregano
2 tablespoons finely chopped parsley
    or finely snipped chives
sea salt and freshly ground black pepper
burger buns, vegan mayonnaise, lettuce,
    sliced gherkins and red onions, to serve
    (optional)
baking sheets lined with baking parchment

Makes 6 burgers

1 tablespoon light olive oil
400 g/14 oz. pumpkin or winter squash,
    peeled, deseeded and chopped into
    2.5-cm/1-in. pieces
400 g/14 oz. pappardelle, tagliatelle
    or any other ribbon pasta
finely grated zest and freshly squeezed
    juice of 1 lemon
50 g/2 oz. wild rocket/arugula leaves
1 large handful of freshly chopped
    flat leaf parsley
sea salt and freshly ground black pepper

RED PEPPER OIL
1 small red (bell) pepper, sliced
6 large red chillies/chiles, sliced
1 small red onion, sliced
4 garlic cloves, peeled but left whole
1 teaspoon cumin seeds
65 ml/¼ cup olive oil

Serves 4

CHUNKY HUMMUS BURGERS

The most fun veggies to use in this recipe are beetroots/beets — they make these burgers bright pink, which makes them, in turn, very popular with kids!

Preheat the oven to 180°C (350°F) Gas 4.

Place the couscous in a bowl, pour over the boiling water, cover and let sit for 5 minutes.

Place all the ingredients in a mixing bowl and knead into a well-combined dough. Divide the mixture into 6 portions and form them into even burgers with your hands. Place them on the lined baking sheet.

Bake in the preheated oven for 20–25 minutes, or until a nice crust forms and the burgers start browning lightly. Here, these are served in a bun with vegan mayonnaise, lettuce, gherkins and red onion. But the trimmings are really up to you!

TAGLIATELLE
WITH PAN-FRIED PUMPKIN & RED PEPPER OIL

The trick to this recipe is to take it slowly. This is contemporary cooking at its best, as it draws on more than one style of cuisine; perfect comfort food.

Preheat the oven to 180°C (350°F) Gas 4. Put the red (bell) pepper, chillies/ chiles, onion, garlic, cumin seeds and 2 tablespoons of the olive oil in a roasting pan. Cook in the preheated oven for 1 hour, turning often. Transfer to a food processor while still hot. Add the remaining oil and whizz until smooth. Let cool, then pour the mixture into a clean and dry screwtop jar.

Heat the light olive oil in a frying pan/skillet set over a high and add the pumpkin. Cook for 10 minutes, turning often, until each piece is golden brown all over. Meanwhile, cook the pasta according to the packet instructions and drain well. Put it in a large bowl and add 2–3 tablespoons of the red pepper oil. Add the cooked pumpkin, lemon zest and juice, rocket/ arugula and parsley and toss to combine. Season well with salt and pepper and serve immediately.

ROASTED AUBERGINE LASAGNE

LENTIL MIXTURE
2 tablespoons olive oil
1 large onion, diced
4 garlic cloves, crushed
250 g/generous 1¼ cups Puy lentils
750 ml/3¼ cups vegetable stock,
    plus extra if needed
12 large tomatoes
1 carrot, diced
1 red (bell) pepper
1 celery stalk, diced
2 tablespoons dark soy sauce
1 bay leaf
handful of fresh marjoram
handful of fresh thyme
2 tablespoons tomato purée/paste
½ teaspoon salt, or to taste
½ teaspoon black pepper, or to taste

AUBERGINE/EGGPLANT LAYER
2 aubergines/eggplants
2 tablespoons olive oil
sea salt and freshly ground black pepper

'BÉCHAMEL'
2 tablespoons olive oil
½ teaspoon salt, or to taste
½ teaspoon white pepper, or to taste
2 tablespoons plain/all-purpose flour
400 ml/scant 1¾ cups almond or soy milk
1 bay leaf
½ teaspoon mustard powder

TO ASSEMBLE
1 packet of egg-free lasagne sheets
120 g/4 oz. grated vegan Italian-style
    hard cheese
sea salt and freshly ground black pepper

Serves 6–8

You can't beat a homemade lasagne. This dish benefits from being left overnight and baked the following day, but a few hours in the fridge will do the job if pushed for time. The lentils can be substituted for vegan 'mince'.

Start with the lentil mixture. Heat 1 tablespoon of the olive oil in a pan and sauté half of the onion and 1 clove of crushed garlic until softened. Add the lentils and sauté for a further minute, then add the stock and simmer until the lentils are fully cooked and soft. Add further stock as needed; you are aiming for the lentils to absorb most of the liquid without leaving too much broth.

Preheat the oven to 210°C (410°F) Gas 6.

Remove the cores from the tomatoes. Place the tomatoes on a baking sheet, along with the remaining crushed garlic and cook in the oven until roasted and almost starting to blacken. Blitz with a hand blender and set aside.

To make the aubergine/eggplant layer, remove the ends of the aubergines/eggplants. Slice them lengthways into 1.5 cm/½ in. thick slices. Place on a baking sheet, drizzle with the olive oil and season. Roast on high heat until golden brown and soft. Set aside.

Reduce the oven to 190°C (375°F) Gas 5.

Back to the lentil mixture. Heat the remaining 1 tablespoon olive oil in a pan and sauté the remaining half of onion, along with the carrot, red (bell) pepper and celery, then add the cooked lentils, soy sauce, bay leaf, the fresh marjoram and thyme. Add the blended tomatoes and the tomato purée/paste. Bring to the boil and simmer for 10 minutes. Add the salt and pepper, then adjust the seasoning according to taste.

To make the 'béchamel', heat the olive oil in small, deep pan, add the salt, white pepper and flour, and cook to make a roux. Gently cook the paste for 2–3 minutes. Slowly add the milk, whisking all the time, until it reaches a creamy sauce consistency. Add the bay leaf and the mustard powder, and simmer for 2–3 minutes. Check the seasoning. Layer some 'béchamel' sauce in the bottom of a large, deep baking dish and cover with lasagne sheets. Add half the lentil and tomato mixture, followed by a layer of aubergine/eggplant, using all the slices and overlapping them to create a thick layer. Add the remaining lentil mixture, a layer of lasagne sheets and top with the 'béchamel'. Sprinkle with vegan cheese, salt and pepper.

Bake for 30–40 minutes until bubbling and the top is golden brown.

SPICY SWEET POTATO MOUSSAKA

One-dish meals are so handy if you're cooking for your family or if you're a fan of prepping your meals for the week ahead. One serving of this moussaka will provide two servings of vegetables in a pretty painless way and doubles up perfectly as lunchbox meals until you've worked through the whole bake.

1 aubergine/eggplant

2 courgettes/zucchini

400 g/3½ cups peeled and diced sweet potato

2 garlic cloves, crushed

½ teaspoon cayenne pepper

½ teaspoon ground chipotle powder

freshly squeezed juice of 1 lime

180 g/1½ cups macadamia nuts, soaked for at least 2 hours

85 g/¾ cup sun-dried tomatoes in oil, drained

1 teaspoon ground cumin

1 tablespoon freshly squeezed lemon juice (or apple cider vinegar)

1 teaspoon salt

2 baking sheets, greased

Serves 8

Preheat the oven to 180°C (350°F) Gas 4.

Slice the aubergine/eggplant and courgette/zucchini into rounds about 1 cm/⅜ in. thick. Arrange on the prepared baking sheets and bake in the preheated oven for 15 minutes. Remove from the oven and set aside to cool, but keep the oven on.

Meanwhile, boil the sweet potato cubes in a large pot of water set over a medium–high heat for about 16 minutes, until soft. Drain and mash the sweet potato and mix in the crushed garlic, cayenne, chipotle powder and lime juice.

Put the macadamia nuts, sun-dried tomatoes, cumin, lemon juice and salt in a blender and pulse until smooth.

Once you have prepared all of the components, it's time to assemble the casserole. Place about 3 tablespoons of the sweet potato mixture at the bottom of the casserole dish and spread thinly – it doesn't matter if it doesn't cover the entire surface. Layer some of the baked aubergine/ eggplant first, then spread a generous layer of the sweet potato mixture on top. Cover this with a layer of courgette/zucchini, then some of the macadamia spread. Repeat until you have used up all of the ingredients, finishing with a thick layer of the macadamia mixture.

Cover the moussaka with foil and bake in the still-warm oven for 20 minutes, then remove the foil and bake for another 15 minutes.

MEDITERRANEAN GREEN LENTIL LOAF

Rich in texture and flavour, this is an ideal choice when your vegan-sceptic friends are visiting for dinner! The lentil and vegetable mixture can be eaten just like that, but it's richer, crispier and more satisfying when baked.

200 g/1 cup dried green lentils, washed and drained

2 bay leaves

4-cm/1½-in. strip of kombu seaweed

½ teaspoon sea salt

3 handfuls of chard, spinach or young kale

5 tablespoons olive oil

6 garlic cloves, crushed

90 g/¾ cup chopped onion

½ teaspoon ground dried rosemary or dried herbes de Provence

2 teaspoons Dijon mustard

2 teaspoons lemon juice

30 g/½ cup almond flour (dried leftovers from making almond milk on pages 10) or 30 g/⅓ cup fine breadcrumbs, plus extra for sprinkling

freshly ground black pepper

12 x 15-cm/4¾ x 6 in. loaf pan, well oiled

Serves 4

In a large saucepan, pour 450 ml/scant 2 cups cold water over the lentils, add the bay leaves and kombu and put on a high heat to boil, uncovered. When the water boils, add 110 ml/scant ½ cup cold water, then reduce the heat to medium, half-cover and continue cooking for about 10 minutes. Add another 110 ml/scant ½ cup cold water, cover the pan fully and simmer for 10 more minutes. Add a final 110 ml/scant ½ cup cold water, cover and simmer for another 10 minutes. The lentils should by now be soft and a little sticky, with no uncooked parts. Add the salt, then take out the bay leaves and kombu, chop up the kombu into small pieces and stir it into the lentils. Blanch the greens in boiling water for a couple of minutes and then drain and chop them.

Heat the olive oil in a frying pan/skillet over a medium heat and then add the garlic, onion, the dried herbs and pepper, to taste. Sauté for a few minutes, then add the blanched greens, cooked lentils, mustard and lemon juice. Mix everything together and then add the flour or breadcrumbs.

Preheat the oven to 200°C (400°F) Gas 6. Add the lentil mix to the oiled loaf pan, making the loaf as high and long as you want. It doesn't have to fill the entire pan. Oil the top with the help of a silicone brush, sprinkle with a little almond flour or a few breadcrumbs and bake for about 30 minutes or until a nice crispy crust forms and the top surface turns golden brown. Let it cool for 20 minutes, then take a big plate and cover the pan with it. With a quick movement, flip the loaf onto the plate. It should retain the shape of the pan. Carefully slice the loaf into thick slices and serve. You can also spoon the mixture out of the pan and serve it like that, if you prefer.

Serve slices of this loaf with Onion Gravy (page 18), mash and a big bowl of garden salad.

PAELLA OF SUMMER VINE VEGETABLES
WITH ALMONDS

This is a meat-free take on the classic Spanish rice dish paella. It's colourful, delicious and bursting with fresh, young vegetables grown on the vine and enhanced with the subtle flavour of saffron. Perfect for summer entertaining.

large pinch of saffron threads
65 ml/¼ cup hot water
80 ml/⅓ cup olive oil
200 g/7 oz. red or yellow
    cherry tomatoes
100 g/3½ oz. green French beans
4 baby courgettes/zucchinis, halved
80 g/3 oz. freshly shelled peas
2 garlic cloves, chopped
2 fresh rosemary sprigs
320 g/11 oz. paella or
    Arborio risotto rice
800 ml/3⅓ cups vegetable stock
30 g/1 oz. flaked/slivered almonds,
    lightly toasted

Serves 4

Put the saffron in a bowl with the hot water and set aside to infuse. Heat half of the oil in a heavy-based frying pan/skillet set over a high heat and add the tomatoes. Cook for 2 minutes, shaking the pan so that the tomatoes soften and start to split. Use a slotted spoon to remove the tomatoes from the pan and set aside. Add the beans, courgettes/zucchinis and peas and stir-fry over a high heat for 2–3 minutes. Set aside with the tomatoes until needed.

Add the remaining oil to the pan with the garlic and rosemary and cook gently for 1 minute to flavour the oil. Add the rice to the pan and cook, stirring constantly, for 2 minutes, until the rice is shiny and opaque. Add the stock and saffron water to the pan. Stir just once or twice, then increase the heat and let the liquid reach the boil. When the stock is rapidly boiling and little holes have formed in the rice, reduce the heat to medium and let simmer gently for about 20 minutes, until almost all the stock has been absorbed.

Scatter the cooked tomatoes, beans, courgettes/zucchinis and peas over the rice, cover lightly with some foil and cook over low heat for 5 minutes so that the vegetables are just heated through. Sprinkle the almonds on top to serve.

MEXICAN VEGETABLE & KIDNEY BEAN BAKE
WITH AVOCADO HOLLANDAISE

1 onion, chopped

3 celery stalks, chopped

2 garlic cloves, finely chopped

3 sweet potatoes, peeled and diced

2 carrots, diced

2 yellow (bell) peppers, deseeded
   and cut into strips

1 red (bell) pepper, deseeded
   and cut into strips

250 g/9 oz. chestnut mushrooms,
   sliced

450 g/1 lb. cherry tomatoes

4–5 tablespoons olive oil

2 teaspoons ground cumin

2 teaspoons ground coriander

2 teaspoons chilli/chili powder

2 teaspoons caster/granulated sugar

600 ml/2½ cups passata/
   strained tomatoes

2 tablespoons good-quality
   tomato ketchup

400-g/14-oz. can red kidney beans,
   drained and rinsed

2 handfuls of fresh baby
   spinach leaves

handful of freshly chopped
   coriander/cilantro

sea salt and freshly ground
   black pepper

AVOCADO HOLLANDAISE

1 large, ripe avocado

freshly squeezed juice of ½ lemon

2 tablespoons olive oil

Serves 4

This is a meat-free chilli/chili that will tempt carnivores, vegetarians and vegans alike. It doesn't pack too much of a punch, making it family-friendly, but chilli/chili-fiends could add some dried chilli/hot red pepper flakes, a slick of the chilli oil, or even a scattering of some freshly chopped chilli/chile. The avocado 'hollandaise' lifts the whole dish to another level, so do make sure to serve the two together.

Preheat the oven to 180°C (350°F) Gas 4. Scatter the onion, celery and garlic into a deep sheet pan.

Add the sweet potatoes, carrots, (bell) peppers, mushrooms and cherry tomatoes to the pan. Drizzle in the olive oil, add the spices and sugar, season with salt and freshly ground black pepper and roast for 30–35 minutes, until the vegetables have started to soften and brown. Remove from the oven and stir in the passata/strained tomatoes and ketchup. Cook for a further 30 minutes. Remove from the oven, stir in the kidney beans, spinach and half of the coriander/cilantro. Return to the oven for about 5 minutes, until the spinach is just wilted. Scatter over the remaining coriander/cilantro.

In the meantime, make the avocado hollandaise. Peel the avocado and remove the pit. Chop the flesh and pop it into the bowl of a blender (alternatively, use a jug/pitcher and a stick blender). Add the lemon juice, 50 ml/3½ tablespoons water and the olive oil and whiz to a smooth purée. Season to taste, transfer to a small bowl and serve alongside the vegetable and kidney bean bake.

TEX-MEX VEGGIE TACOS
WITH FRESH TOMATO SALSA & CHIPOTLE MAYONNAISE

1 large sweet potato, peeled and cut into chunks

1 small butternut squash, peeled, deseeded and cut into chunks

1 red (bell) pepper, deseeded and diced

2 corn on the cob/ears of corn

4 tablespoons olive oil

2 garlic cloves, grated

1 tablespoon paprika

1 tablespoon freshly chopped rosemary

400-g/14-oz. can red kidney beans

8 crunchy taco shells

small bunch of freshly chopped parsley

2 handfuls of shredded iceberg lettuce, to serve

TOMATO SALSA

200 g/7 oz. cherry tomatoes

1 small red onion

juice of 1 lime

a small bunch of freshly chopped coriander/cilantro

a handful of fresh mint leaves, roughly torn

CHIPOTLE MAYONNAISE

2 teaspoons chipotle paste

1 quantity tofu mayonnaise (see page 14)

Serves 4

This dish is a riot of colour, flavours and textures. You could fill the tacos before you serve them, but it creates such a lovely, relaxed dining experience when you lay everything out so that everyone can dive in and fill their own.

Preheat the oven to 190°C (375°F) Gas 5. Scatter the sweet potato, butternut squash and (bell) pepper over the base of a large sheet pan. Stand the corn cobs/ears on a board and remove the corn using a sharp knife and a downward motion. Scatter the sweetcorn/corn kernels over the vegetables in the pan. Drizzle everything with the olive oil, sprinkle in the grated garlic, paprika and freshly chopped rosemary. Transfer to the oven and roast for about 25 minutes, until the sweet potato and squash are soft.

Remove the pan from the oven. Drain and rinse the kidney beans and add to the vegetables, then push everything up the pan slightly, so that you can tuck the taco shells across one end. Return the pan to the oven for about 3–4 minutes, until the tacos are crisp and the beans are heated through.

Stir the chopped parsley into the vegetables.

For the tomato salsa, coarsely chop the tomatoes and put them into a bowl. Peel and thinly slice the onion and stir it into the tomatoes. Squeeze in the lime juice and add the coriander/cilantro and torn mint leaves.

For the chipotle mayonnaise, mix the chipotle paste and mayonnaise together.

Place a little shredded lettuce into the base of each taco, pile with the vegetable mix and some salsa, then drizzle with a little chipotle mayonnaise – or lay everything out on a platter and invite everyone to fill their own.

STUFFED & ROASTED BUTTERNUT SQUASH

This recipe takes advantage of the sturdy yet tender texture of butternut squash when baked. Presented stuffed, it makes a great centrepiece for the table and looks great cut into slices. The sweet, mellow flavour of the squash is complemented by feta-style vegan cheese.

1 butternut squash

4 tablespoons olive oil

1 small red onion, thinly sliced

2 garlic cloves, crushed

100 g/3½ oz. cooked Puy lentils

100 g/3½ oz. cooked mixed grains

150 ml/⅔ cup vegetable stock

3 sprigs fresh thyme, leaves picked

1 tablespoon Dijon mustard

50 g/2 oz. feta-style vegan cheese, crumbled or chopped

30 g/⅓ cup sun-dried tomatoes, chopped

2 tablespoons chopped walnuts

1 fennel bulb, thinly sliced (optional)

small handful of freshly chopped parsley

sea salt and freshly ground black pepper

steamed Tenderstem broccoli, to serve

cooking string/twine

Serves 6

Preheat the oven to 180°C (350°F) Gas 4.

Cut the butternut squash in half lengthways. Scoop out and discard the seeds, then put both halves in a roasting pan, cut-side up. Drizzle 1 tablespoon of the olive oil on top of each squash half and rub around to coat. Roast in the preheated oven for 20–25 minutes until the squash is just tender when pierced with a fork. The timing may vary a little depending on the size of your squash. Be careful not to overcook the squash as it will be cooked again when assembled.

Remove the squash from the oven and leave to cool long enough so that you can handle it. Scoop out and set aside the flesh in the centre of both halves, leaving about a 2.5-cm/1-in. border all around so that the vegetable keeps its shape. Roughly dice the removed squash flesh and set aside for a moment.

In a large frying pan/skillet, heat 1 tablespoon of the oil over a medium-high heat. When hot, sauté the onion and garlic for about 10 minutes until softened and beginning to brown. Add the cooked Puy lentils and cooked grains, then add the vegetable stock and cook for a further 5 minutes, stirring occasionally.

Remove the pan from the heat and add the thyme leaves, mustard, vegan cheese, sun-dried tomatoes, walnuts and fennel (if using). Season with salt and pepper and mix well. Finally, stir in the chopped squash flesh and parsley. Stuff the mixture into both sides of the roasted squash, packing it down so that you can fit in as much as possible.

Pick up one squash half and quickly and carefully turn it upside-down on top of the other half. Use the kitchen string/twine to tie up the squash to keep it together. (You can now choose to let the squash cool, cover with foil and store in the fridge for up to 3 days until ready to cook, or you can roast it straight away.)

When ready, lightly brush the squash with the remaining 1 tablespoon oil. Bake in the preheated oven for 20–35 minutes to heat through.

FRESH LIME, VEGETABLE & COCONUT CURRY

CURRY PASTE
45 g/1½ oz. piece of fresh root
  ginger, peeled
2 garlic cloves, peeled
1 stalk lemongrass, trimmed
3 kaffir lime leaves
1 tablespoon ground coriander
1 tablespoon ground cumin
1 scant tablespoon dried chilli/
  red pepper flakes
1 tablespoon coconut oil
1–2 tablespoons warm water
a bunch of fresh coriander/cilantro

CURRY
2 x 400-ml/14-fl. oz. cans
  full-fat coconut milk
100 ml/⅓ cup plus 1 tablespoon
  well-flavoured vegetable stock
1 tablespoon demerara/
  turbinado sugar
100 g/3½ oz. cherry tomatoes,
  roughly chopped
1 yellow (bell) pepper, deseeded
  and cut into strips
400 g/14 oz. mixed young vegetables
  (sugar snap peas, green/French
  beans, young, long-stem broccoli,
  baby corn, etc.)
small bunch of fresh coriander/
  cilantro, roughly chopped
zest and juice of 1 large lime

TO SERVE
handful of cashew nuts
bunch of spring onions/scallions,
  thinly sliced

Serves 4

More often than not, standard Thai curry pastes usually contain dried shrimps or fish sauce. This recipe uses a delicious and easily made alternative paste. It helps if you have a food processor, or mini chopper, but you could also make the paste using a pestle and mortar. The vegetables don't need to be cooked for too long.

To make the curry paste, roughly chop the ginger, garlic and lemongrass and add them to a food processor or mini chopper and whiz until finely chopped (or bash them using a pestle and mortar if preferred). Add the lime leaves, ground coriander, cumin, chilli/red pepper flakes and coconut oil. Pour in the warm water and blitz everything to a paste. Add the coriander/cilantro and whiz again until everything is ground down and evenly mixed.

Preheat the oven to 180°C (350°F) Gas 4. For the curry, pour the coconut milk and stock into a deep roasting pan and stir in the curry paste and sugar. Cover with foil and cook for 15 minutes.

Remove the roasting pan from the oven, give everything a good stir and add the chopped tomatoes, (bell) pepper strips and prepared vegetables (cut the baby corn in half from top to bottom, if using). Replace the foil and cook for 10 minutes or so, until the vegetables are just soft but retain their bright colours.

Stir in the fresh coriander/cilantro and add the lime zest and juice. Serve straight away, scattered with cashews and spring onions/scallions.

½ green cabbage, cut into thick slices

½ red cabbage, cut into thick slices

5 plums, pitted and cut into wedges

2 red onions, cut into wedges

2 tablespoons flavourless oil

PLUM SAUCE

1 thumb-sized piece of fresh root ginger

150 g/¾ cup soft light brown sugar

150 ml/⅔ cup apple cider vinegar

1 tablespoon freshly squeezed lemon juice

1 teaspoon sea salt

1 teaspoon Chinese five-spice powder

½ teaspoon chilli flakes/
    hot red pepper flakes

2 baking pans, lined with baking parchment

STICKY PLUM-ROASTED CABBAGES

Preheat the oven to 180°C (350°F) Gas 4.

Peel and finely grate the ginger. Combine all the plum sauce ingredients in a small saucepan over a low-medium heat, stirring occasionally, for 10–15 minutes until the sugar and spices have dissolved and you have a smooth sauce.

Arrange the cabbage slices, plums and red onion on the prepared baking pans and drizzle evenly with the oil and then the sauce, reserving a little sauce to serve on the side of the dish.

Roast in the preheated oven for 25–30 minutes.

The cabbages should be browned and sticky but still have some bite when cooked. Serve with the reserved plum sauce on the side.

2 x 200 g/7 oz. blocks firm tofu, drained
    and excess water pressed out

cooking oil spray

2 teaspoons sea salt

1 teaspoon onion powder

1 tablespoon Sichuan pepper

pinch of cayenne pepper

½ teaspoon chilli/chili powder

baking sheet, lined with baking parchment

TOFU CHIPS

Preheat the oven to 150°C (300°F) Gas 2.

Slice the tofu into very thin pieces. Lay out the slices on the prepared baking sheet. Lightly mist the slices with a little cooking spray. Bake in the preheated oven for about 25 minutes or until golden brown and crisp.

Mix together the remaining ingredients in a small bowl and sprinkle on the tofu chips to taste, then serve.

300 g/10 ½ oz. green/French beans

150 g/generous 1 cup raw cashews

1 tablespoon soy sauce

4 tablespoons rice vinegar

1 garlic clove, crushed

1 thumb-sized piece of fresh ginger,
    peeled and grated

1 teaspoon toasted sesame oil

1 teaspoon white sugar

sea salt

GREEN BEANS & GLAZED CASHEWS

Bring a large pan of salted water to the boil. Add the green/French beans and bring back to the boil, then simmer for about 3–4 minutes until just tender. Drain and plunge straight into a bowl of ice-cold water to stop the cooking process. Drain the beans well and dry with paper towels. Set aside.

Dry-toast the cashews in a small frying pan/skillet over a medium heat, shaking the pan to make sure they don't burn. Once toasted, turn the heat up to medium-high and add the soy sauce. Toss to coat and cook for about 30 seconds until the liquid has evaporated. Leave to cool.

In a large bowl, whisk together the rice vinegar, garlic, ginger, sesame oil and sugar. Add the green/French beans to the dressing and stir to coat. Serve topped with the soy-glazed cashews.

SWEET THINGS

OAT BARS FILLED WITH JAM

Home-baked bars are so easy to make and you'll be very grateful to find them in your cupboard whenever you crave sweets or need a takeaway breakfast or healthy snack.

300 g/3 cups rolled/old-fashioned oats
130 g/1 cup unbleached spelt flour
½ teaspoon bourbon vanilla powder
½ teaspoon ground cinnamon
1 teaspoon baking powder
½ teaspoon salt
170 g/⅔ cup brown rice syrup
130 g/½ cup coconut or sunflower oil
90 g/4 tablespoons naturally sweetened fruit jam

23 x 30-cm/9 x 12-in. baking pan, greased

Makes 12

Preheat the oven to 180°C (350°F) Gas 4.

Mix the oats, flour, vanilla powder, cinnamon, baking powder and salt in a mixing bowl, then add the syrup and oil and mix thoroughly with a wooden spoon.

Spoon half the dough into the prepared baking pan and press down evenly into the pan. Spread the fruit preserve over the dough with a wet spatula, then spoon over the remaining dough, smoothing the top with a spatula.

Bake in the preheated oven for 20 minutes. Remove from the baking pan and allow to cool on a wire rack.

Cut into squares to serve. Refrigerated, they'll keep for 2 weeks in an airtight container but it's more likely they'll be gone in 2 days!

Variation You could also try filling these with hazelnut or carob spread.

BAY-SCENTED HASSELBACK ORCHARD FRUITS
WITH CINNAMON MAPLE GLAZE

Fresh bay leaves add a heavenly flavour and scent to this lovely dish. They make a really pretty dessert – perfect with a coconut rice pudding.

3 ripe, but firm pears
3 crunchy eating apples
100 ml/⅓ cup plus 1 tablespoon maple syrup, plus extra to serve
1 teaspoon ground cinnamon
freshly squeezed juice of 1 orange
about 15–20 fresh bay leaves

Serves 4

Preheat the oven to 180°C (350°F) Gas 4. Peel the pears and apples, and cut them in half. Cut them into thin slices, without going all the way through.

Stir the maple syrup, ground cinnamon and orange juice together and brush this over the fruit, making sure to get lots of the mixture in between the slices. Cut the bay leaves in half along their length from stalk to tip and gently push them in between some of the slices in the fruit. Cook for 25 minutes, basting halfway through, and then pouring over any leftover glaze 5 minutes before the end of the cooking time.

Drizzle with extra maple syrup to serve, if desired.

GRAIN-FREE CHOCOLATE NOUGAT BAR

190 g/2 cups almond flour
2 tablespoons coconut flour
1 teaspoon vanilla bean powder
120 ml/¹/₂ cup melted coconut oil
2 tablespoons lucuma powder

CARAMEL
125 g/¹/₂ cup almond butter, softened
75 ml/¹/₃ cup melted coconut oil
75 ml/¹/₃ cup maple syrup
¹/₄ teaspoon sea salt
1 teaspoon vanilla bean powder

CHOCOLATE
60 ml/¹/₄ cup melted coconut oil
25 g/¹/₄ cup cacao powder
2 tablespoons maple syrup
pinch of sea salt
2 tablespoons maca powder

brownie pan lined with parchment paper

Makes 16 bars

These caramel-and-chocolate covered bars – remiscient of the popular
Twix – include nutrient-rich lucuma and maca.

Preheat the oven to 180°C (350°F) Gas 4. To make the shortbread, put all the
ingredients in a bowl and mix until well combined. Pour the mixture into the
prepared pan and press it into the bottom of the pan. Bake in the oven for
11–13 minutes, or until the sides of the shortbread are lightly brown. Let cool.

Next, make the caramel. Put all the ingredients in a bowl and mix until
completely smooth. Pour over the cooled shortbread and chill in the
refrigerator for 1–2 hours, until the caramel has hardened.

To prepare the chocolate mixture, put all the ingredients in a bowl and mix
until smooth. Pour the chocolate over the caramel layer chill in the
refrigerator for 1 hour, or until hardened.

To remove from the pan, lift it up using the parchment paper and place it
on a cutting board. Cut into 16 bars. The bars will keep for up to 1 week in
an airtight container in the refrigerator or 1 month in the freezer.

VEGAN MAPLE CHOC NUT FUDGE

60 g/2¹/₄ oz. dark/bittersweet dairy-free
    chocolate, about 70% cocoa solids,
    broken into even-sized pieces
2 tablespoons tahini
25 g/1 oz. raw cacao butter
2 tablespoons maple syrup
100 g/3¹/₂ oz. sesame seeds
100 g/3¹/₂ oz. macadamia nuts
¹/₄ teaspoon ground cinnamon

*brownie pan, lined with parchment
    paper leaving enough overhang
    to cover the top*

Makes 24

The combination of tahini, raw cacao butter and macadamia nuts adds
a real creaminess to this fudge without the need for dairy products.

Put the dark/bittersweet chocolate, tahini, cacao butter and maple syrup in a
heatproof bowl. Place over a pan of simmering water (make sure the bottom
of the bowl does not touch the water) and heat gently until everything is
melted, giving the mixture an occasional stir. Leave to cool slightly.

Blitz the sesame seeds and macadamia nuts in a food processor until they are
very finely chopped and turning buttery. Spoon the blended seeds and nuts
into the melted chocolate mixture, add the cinnamon and stir until combined.
Spoon the chocolate mixture into the lined brownie pan and smooth with
the back of a dampened spoon into an even layer, about 2 cm/³/₄ in. thick.
Fold the overhanging parchment paper over the top. Freeze for 1 hour
or until firm, then lift out of the pan using the paper to help and cut into
24 squares. Store in the fridge in an airtight container for up to 2 weeks.

PEANUT BUTTER QUINOA COOKIES

420 g/1¾ cup creamy peanut butter
75 g/¾ cup xylitol or other sugar substitute
140 ml/¾ cup agave syrup
2 tablespoons ground flaxseed combined
    with 6 tablespoons water
1 teaspoon pure vanilla extract
45 g/½ cup quinoa flakes
2 tablespoons quinoa flour
½ teaspoon bicarbonate of soda/
    baking soda

a baking sheet lined with parchment paper

Makes 24

These are good – really good. They use quinoa in its flake and flour form, so are full of goodness. They won't last for very long.

Preheat the oven to 180°C (350°F) Gas 4.

Mix all ingredients together in a large mixing bowl. Once the ingredients are all combined, bring the mixture together in your hands then roll into 2.5-cm/1-in. balls and place onto the prepared baking sheet. Using your thumb, press down each ball so it is slightly flattened out.

You can use your fingers for this which is great for getting children involved too.

Bake in the preheated oven for approximately 12 minutes, until the cookies are golden, and serve warm. Store the cookies in an airtight container for up to 3 days.

DROP COOKIES WITH PERSIMMON & CRANBERRIES

70 g/½ cup coconut oil
    or vegan margarine, at room
    temperature
170 g/⅔ cup brown rice syrup
250 ml/1 cup persimmon pulp from
    1–2 persimmons), pushed through
    a sieve/strainer
60 g/½ cup chopped walnuts
60 g/½ cup dried cranberries
200 g/1½ cups unbleached
    plain/all-purpose flour
60 g/½ cup unbleached spelt or plain
    wholemeal/whole-wheat flour
2 teaspoons baking powder
½ teaspoon ground cinnamon
¼ teaspoon salt
plain soy milk, as needed

baking sheets, lined with baking parchment

Makes about 26

Japanese persimmon or kaki is a sweet fruit with a soft texture. It is a species native to China but is now widely spread throughout the Mediterranean too. Allow the fruits to ripen and soften to bring out their best flavour.

Preheat the oven to 180°C (350°F) Gas 4.

In a large mixing bowl, beat together the coconut oil or margarine, the syrup and persimmon pulp. Add the walnuts and cranberries and stir through. Sift the flours, baking powder, cinnamon and salt into the bowl and stir in with a wooden spoon.

If the dough seems too dry, add a splash of milk but not too much – the dough should be thick enough not to slide off the spoon.

Drop generous tablespoons of the dough onto the prepared baking sheets, about 1 cm/½ in. apart. Bake the cookies in the preheated oven for 15 minutes.

Remove the cookies from the oven and allow to cool on the baking sheets. Store in an airtight container for up to 2 weeks.

BEAN & CASHEW BROWNIES

At first, the idea of using cooked beans in a brownie mixture might not sound too promising or appealing. However, blended beans give a wonderful texture to the brownies and it's a great way to introduce plant protein to kids or people who wouldn't want to eat a bean stew.

300 g/2 cups canned unsalted haricot/navy beans (see method for an alternative)
200 g/1½ cups finely chopped vegan dark/bittersweet chocolate, about 70% cocoa solids
65 g/⅓ cup sunflower oil
130 g/½ cup brown rice or pure maple syrup
freshly squeezed juice and grated zest of 1 lemon
80 g/½ cup whole or 80 g/1 cup finely ground cashews
85 g/⅔ cup unbleached plain/all-purpose flour
40 g/⅓ cup plain wholemeal/whole-wheat flour
1 tablespoon baking powder
¼ teaspoon salt
¼ teaspoon ground cinnamon
2 tablespoons apricot jam, to serve

23 x 30-cm/9 x 12-in. baking pan, oiled

Makes about 20

If you want to cook the haricot/navy beans from scratch, soak 140 g/¾ cup dried beans in a lot of water overnight. Drain, cover with three times the volume of water and cook for 1 hour (or 40 minutes in a pressure cooker). Drain well.

Preheat the oven to 180°C (350°F) Gas 4.

Melt the chocolate in a heatproof bowl set over a saucepan of simmering water. Do not let the base of the bowl touch the water.

Put the melted chocolate, cooked beans, oil, syrup, lemon juice and zest in a food processor and blend until smooth.

If using whole cashews, finely grind them in a food processor or spice mill. Mix the flours, ground cashews, baking powder, salt and cinnamon in a mixing bowl. Add the bean mixture and fold in with a spatula until you get a smooth, thick consistency (much thicker than usual cake mixtures).

Spoon the cake mixture into the prepared baking pan and spread level with a spatula; if it sticks too much, wet it with warm water and try again. Bake in the preheated oven for 15–20 minutes. Do not overbake – they are supposed to be a little gooey! Allow to cool completely in the baking pan.

Cut into squares to serve. Serve with a little apricot jam/jelly, which contrasts beautifully with the rich, heavy chocolate taste of these brownies.

BLACK-FOREST-GÂTEAU CUPCAKES

130 g/1 cup unbleached plain/
   all-purpose flour
65 g/½ cup plain wholemeal/
   whole-wheat flour
80 g/½ cup semolina/farina
45 g/½ cup cocoa powder
2 teaspoons baking powder
1 teaspoon bicarbonate of/
   baking soda
¼ teaspoon salt
100 g/½ cup sunflower oil
260 g/1 cup brown rice syrup
170 ml/¾ cup plain soy milk
1 teaspoon freshly squeezed
   lemon juice
grated zest of 2 lemons
60 g/½ cup chopped vegan
   dark/bittersweet chocolate
360 g/1½ cups cherries in Kirsch
1 teaspoon arrowroot powder
whipped soy cream, to decorate

CHOCOLATE FROSTING

130 g/1 cup finely chopped vegan
   dark/bittersweet chocolate
50 ml/scant ¼ cup non-dairy milk
2 tablespoons brown rice syrup

*12-hole muffin pan lined with
   paper cupcake cases*

Makes 12

Schwarzwald, or Black-Forest cake is so very popular and this vegan version of it, made into cupcakes, will be no exception! The chocolate-cherry-whipped-cream combination is a winner and this recipe is so much tastier than other Schwarzwald desserts!

Preheat the oven to 180°C (350°F) Gas 4.

Mix together the flours, semolina/farina, cocoa powder, baking powder, bicarbonate of/baking soda and salt in a bowl.

In a separate bowl, mix together the oil, syrup, milk, lemon juice and zest. Pour into the bowl of dry ingredients and mix gently with a wooden spoon until just incorporated. Fold in the chocolate.

Divide the cake mixture between the muffin cases.

Bake in the preheated oven for 20–25 minutes. Allow to cool for a few minutes, then remove the cupcakes from the muffin pan and allow to cool completely on a wire rack.

For the chocolate frosting, melt the chocolate in a heatproof bowl set over a saucepan of simmering water. Do not let the base of the bowl touch the water. Meanwhile, heat the milk in a pan until just before boiling. Pour the melted chocolate into the hot milk and whisk until smooth. Add the syrup and mix well. Allow to cool for 45 minutes or until set.

Drain the cherries, saving the Kirsch. Mix the arrowroot into a couple of teaspoons of cold water, then stir into the reserved Kirsch in a pan. Set over a medium heat and whisk until it thickens a little – about 2 minutes.

Scoop a little well out of the top of each cooled cupcake with a teaspoon. Carefully pour about 1 teaspoon Kirsch syrup in each well. Place a cherry in there too. Briefly whisk the cooled chocolate frosting, then spread over the cupcakes. Spoon a dollop of whipped soy cream onto each cupcake, top with a couple of cherries and a drizzle of the Kirsch syrup. Serve immediately!

CHEESECAKE & SWEET CHERRIES

Achieving that cloying, deeply creamy goodness of a cheesecake without dairy takes some work. There are a number of ways you can get excellent results using cashews or silken tofu, but for a cheesecake that no one will know is dairy free, the 'Tofutti' brand of dairy-free cream cheese is the answer. Made from soy and non-hydrogenated vegetable oils, it is identical to normal cream cheese in taste and texture, especially in this glorious dessert.

500 g/1 lb. fresh cherries, pitted
4 tablespoons agave syrup

BASE
150 g/1 cup pecans
150 g/5 oz. Scottish oatcakes
80 g/5½ tablespoons coconut oil
2 tablespoons agave syrup
good pinch of sea salt

FILLING
900 g/1 lb. 14 oz. Tofutti
   Cream Cheese
grated zest of 5 lemons
   and juice of 1
130 g/¾ cup xylitol
5 eggs
1 tablespoon rice flour
2 teaspoons pure vanilla extract
pinch of sea salt

*20-cm/8-in. springform pan,
   lined with baking parchment*

Serves 10–12

Preheat the oven to 180°C (350°F) Gas 4.

To make the base, roast the pecans on a baking sheet in the preheated oven for 10 minutes or until they have gone a shade darker. Allow to cool slightly and leave the oven on.

Melt the coconut oil in a pan over the lowest heat possible – this will only take a few moments. Crush the oatcakes and roasted pecans in a food processor or in a sealed bag with a rolling pin, then transfer to a bowl with the melted coconut oil, agave syrup and salt and mix very well. Press into the baking pan so that you have an even and smooth base for the cheesecake.

To make the filling, put all the ingredients in a food processor and blitz until well combined. Pour the mixture onto the set cheesecake base and smooth out the top. Bake for about 45 minutes or until it is just set and the middle is still a little wobbly. It will set further as it cools. Once completely cold, pop the cheesecake out of the baking pan and peel off the paper.

To serve, squash the cherries a little between your hands to release some of the juices. Add the agave syrup and mix together. Just before serving, pour onto the middle of the cheesecake and serve big wedges with the cherry liquid seeping down the sides.

RICH CARROT CAKE

200 g/1½ cups unbleached
    plain/all-purpose flour
65 g/½ cup plain wholemeal/
    whole-wheat flour
1 teaspoon baking powder
1 teaspoon bicarbonate of/
    baking soda
¼ teaspoon salt
1 teaspoon ground cinnamon
40 g/1 cup desiccated coconut
½ teaspoon bourbon vanilla powder
100 g/½ cup coconut oil
170 g/⅔ cup pure maple syrup
freshly squeezed juice and grated
    zest of 1 orange, plus extra
    to decorate
½ teaspoon apple cider vinegar
1 teaspoon rum
330 g/3 cups grated carrots
60 g/½ cup raisins
80 g/½ cup chopped walnuts

FROSTING
220 ml/1 cup oat milk
2 tablespoons oat or soy cream
3 tablespoons pure maple syrup
3 scant tablespoons cornflour/
    cornstarch
½ teaspoon bourbon vanilla powder
6 drops of pure orange extract
    or 1 tablespoon finely grated
    orange zest

*23-cm/9-in. springform cake pan,
baselined with baking parchment
and oiled*

Serves about 8

This recipe contains all of the expected ingredients (carrots, walnuts, raisins) but it is sweetened with maple syrup, it's low in fat and the frosting is very light.

Preheat the oven to 180°C (350°F) Gas 4.

Sift together the flours, baking powder, bicarbonate of/baking soda, salt and cinnamon in a bowl, add the desiccated coconut and vanilla powder and mix well.

If the coconut oil has solidified, put the jar in a bowl of hot water until the oil has softened.

In a separate bowl, mix together the syrup, coconut oil, orange juice and zest, vinegar and rum.

Combine both bowls and mix until smooth. Add the carrots, raisins and walnuts and fold in with a spatula. The mixture will be thicker than a normal cake mixture.

Spoon the cake mixture into the prepared cake pan and spread level with a spatula. Bake in the preheated oven for 30 minutes. Allow to cool completely in the pan.

For the frosting, put all the ingredients in a small saucepan and whisk well for the cornflour/cornstarch to dissolve. Set over medium heat and whisk vigorously for a couple of minutes. As the milk starts to warm up, the cornflour/cornstarch will start to thicken it. As soon as the frosting is thick enough to spread, remove it from the heat.

Remove the cake from the pan and spread the hot frosting over the top with a spatula. Allow to cool completely.

Decorate the cake with orange zest and drizzle a little maple syrup on each slice to make it sweeter, if you like.

IN ADVANCE
3 ripe bananas

FOR BERRY ICE-CREAM,
add to the sliced bananas
160 g/1¼ cups frozen or fresh raspberries,
sour-cherries, etc.
¼ teaspoon bourbon vanilla powder
2 tablespoons agave syrup

FOR DOUBLE COCOA ICE-CREAM,
add to the sliced bananas
2 tablespoons raw cocoa powder
2 tablespoons agave syrup
¼ teaspoon ground cinnamon
1 tablespoon raw cocoa nibs
(mix in after blending)

**FOR DOUBLE CAPUCINO-HAZELNUT
ICE-CREAM,** add to the sliced bananas
2 tablespoons grain coffee powder
1 teaspoon coffee extract
2 tablespoons maple syrup
¼ teaspoon bourbon vanilla powder
4 tablespoons dry-roasted hazelnuts,
chopped (mix in after blending)

All recipes serve 2

COOKIE
250 g/1½ cups almonds
150 g/1½ cups dates
30 g/¼ cup raw cacao powder
1 tablespoon coconut oil

ICE CREAM
2 frozen bananas
large handful of frozen cherries
pinch of salt
*baking sheet, greased and lined
with baking parchment*

Makes 8

THE QUICKEST & YUMMIEST ICE-CREAM

This type of ice-cream is very popular with raw foodies, but becomes an instant favourite with anybody who tries it. Here are three great combinations made with the same base, i.e. fully ripe frozen bananas!

Peel the bananas and put them together in a bag. Put the bag in the freezer and freeze them until they're completely hard. Take out of the freezer 10 minutes before using.

Slice the frozen bananas with a sharp knife. Place the banana slices and all other ingredients for that particular ice-cream in a high-speed blender. Blend on the high setting and use the tamper (a tool that comes with the blender, which is used to push the ingredients down into the blades) to accelerate the blending process.

You might be able to make these ice-creams in a food processor, too, but it will probably take longer and turn out on the softer side because of the longer blending time. Serve immediately!

CAVEMAN ICE CREAM SANDWICHES

These cherry-chocolate ice cream sandwiches are basically the Fred Flintstone version — fruit, nuts, coconut oil and cacao only.

Put all of the cookie ingredients in a food processor and pulse until smooth and a ball starts to form. Spread out to about 2.5 cm/1 in. thick on the prepared baking sheet. Put in the freezer to set for at least 20 minutes. Remove from the freezer once it has hardened and cut into 16 small squares.

Rinse the food processor and pulse all of the ice cream ingredients together until they resemble the texture of ice cream. Scoop 2 heaped tablespoons of ice cream onto half of the cookie squares and top each with another cookie, so that you have 6 sandwiches. Press the cookies together and use a knife to smooth out the ice cream filling, if necessary. Store the sandwiches in the freezer until you are ready to serve, removing 5–10 minutes before serving.

COCONUT CHIA PUDDING

40 g/¼ cup chia seeds
1 teaspoon pure vanilla extract
¼ teaspoon coconut extract
  (available online)
1 tablespoon cashew butter
300 ml/1¼ cup coconut milk
1 teaspoon ground cinnamon
2 tablespoons shredded coconut,
  plus 1 tablespoon, to decorate
2 tablespoons jam, to serve (optional)

Serves 2

This guilt-free dessert is a great alternative to a traditional rice pudding. Cashew butter gives this dessert a subtle warmth, but peanut butter and is just as delicious!

Put the chia seeds aside in a large mixing bowl. Mix the rest of the ingredients together in a food processor. Then pour the mixture into the mixing bowl with the chia seeds and stir with a fork. Set aside and then stir again after 10 minutes.

Put in the refrigerator to set. The pudding will be firm after an hour but can be left to set overnight.

When ready to serve, sprinkle shredded coconut over each pudding and add a dollop of your favourite fruit jam.

CHAI-GINGER PANNA COTTA

1 teaspoon agar powder
375 ml/1½ cups coconut milk
115 g/⅓ cup maple syrup
1 teaspoon pure vanilla extract
1 teaspoon chai spice
½ tablespoon grated fresh ginger

TO SERVE
4 tablespoons coconut chips
2 tablespoons coconut oil
1 banana, thinly sliced
2 tablespoons coconut sugar
pinch of ground cinnamon
½ tablespoon freshly squeezed
  lemon juice

4 ramekins

Serves 4

Chai and ginger together is such an irresistible pairing. Here, it's used to give an old classic a modern twist.

Gently whisk the agar with 125 ml/½ cup of the coconut milk in a small saucepan or pot. Set over a medium heat and simmer gently for 3–5 minutes to dissolve the agar, taking care not to let the mixture boil. Once dissolved, stir in the remaining coconut milk, the maple syrup, vanilla extract, chai spice and ginger. Warm through for about 5 minutes.

Pour the mixture into the ramekins and put in the fridge to cool and set for at least 4 hours.

Before serving, toast the coconut chips in a dry frying pan/skillet set over a medium heat, until browned. Transfer to a plate to cool, then, using the same pan, warm the coconut oil. When the coconut oil begins to bubble, add the sliced banana to the pan and throw in the coconut sugar and cinnamon. Cook for 2–3 minutes to caramelize the banana.

Remove the panna cottas from the fridge, flip them over onto dessert plates and top with the caramelized banana and toasted coconut chips.

Add the lemon juice to the pan, stir and pour over the panna cottas.

INDEX

RECIPE CREDITS

Jordan & Jessica Bourke
Bircher muesli
Butternut squash falafels with fig, chioggia
  beetroot & chilli oil
Cheesecake & sweet cherries
Granola
Wild mushroom & leek risotto

Chloe Coker & Jane Montgomery
Caponata

Ross Dobson
Aubergine, tomato & red lentil curry
Grilled mixed vegetable platter with soy glaze
Paella of summer vine vegetables with
  almonds
Spiced cauliflower soup
Sweet potato & coconut soup with Thai pesto
Tagliatelle with pan-fried pumpkin & red
  pepper oil

Amy Ruth Finegold
Coconut chia pudding
Lentil & squash soup
Peanut butter quinoa cookies
Quinoa burgers with portabello mushrooms
Quinoa soup with red beans & kale
Roasted asparagus & farro soup
Shredded carrot & courgette salad with miso
  sauce
Wild rice with artichoke, peaches & pine nuts

Liz Franklin
Bay-scented hasselback orchard fruits
Chickpea & almond curry
Cinnamon spiced bruschetta
Crushed butter beans with roasted
  tomatoes and avocado
Ethiopian lentil casserole
Fresh lime, vegetable & coconut curry
Mexican vegetable & kidney bean bake with
  avocado hollandaise
Potato & rosemary pizza
Sticky sesame aubergine with gochujang
  ketchup
Tex-mex veggie tacos

Nicola Graimes
Amaranth & green lentil salad with za'atar
Cajun tortilla chips
Char-grilled asparagus with herb oil
Freekeh, pumpkin & crispy ginger salad
Grain-free 'cheesy' pumpkin crackers
Japanese wakame, radish & edamame salad
Kamut with chermoula dressing
Kimchi, avocado & alfalfa salad and Asian slaw
Long-stem broccoli with lemon-mustard
  dressing
Red quinoa tabbouleh
Rice noodle & smoked tofu salad

Roasted vegetable salad with tapenade
  dressing
Shoots, flowers & leaves
Vegan maple choc nut fudge

Dunja Gulin
Alkalizing green guice
Almond & cashew nut cheese
Bean & cashew brownies
Black forest gateau cupcakes
Caramelized carrot hummus
Carrot juice with beets and pomegranate
Chapatis
Chunky hummus burgers
Coconut & strawberry frappe
Drop cookies with persimmon & cranberries
Grilled tempeh baguette
Healing azuki bean stew with amaranth
Hearty miso soup
Hummus
Mediterranean green lentil loaf
Nut & seed milk
Oat bars filled with jam
Onion gravy and stif-fry sauce
Raw cocoa milk shake
Rich carrot cake
Rye crackers with chia seeds
Seed falafel
Spicy oat cookies with cashews
Stuffed courgettes
Sunflower & cashew mayonnaise
Sweet tahini 'butter' spread
Tahini popcorn
The quickest Ice cream
Tofu mayonnaise
Vegan stuffing

Jackie Kearney
Roasted aubergine lasagne
Vegan fish sauce

Kathy Kordalis
Cauliflower larb with coconut rice & fresh
  leaves
Quick cauliflower rice with saffron pilaf
Sticky plum-roasted cabbages with green
  beans & glazed cashews & tofu chips
Stuffed & roasted butternut squash
Thai green cauli curry
Ultimate veggie roast

Noelle Renée Kovary
Grain-free chocolate nougat bar

Hannah Miles
Baked potato with artichoke and olive
  rocket salad
Baked potato with grilled leeks & romesco
  sauce

Shelagh Ryan
Smashed avocado on toast
Strawberry, banana & almond smoothie bowl

Jenny Tschiesche
Chickpea & pepper curry bake
Quinoa tabbouleh
Ratatouille baked beans
Roasted summer vegetables
Simple Thai vegetables

Jenna Zoe
Açai bowl
Caveman ice cream sandwiches
Chai-ginger panna cotta
Chilli-cheese butternut squash fries
Green energy soup
Hot spinach & artichoke dip
Macadamia nut cheese
Not-your-average wrap
Oodles of zoodles
Spicy green papaya salad
Spicy sweet potato moussaka
Sweet nut butters
Waldorf salad

PHOTOGRAPHY CREDITS

Susan Bell Page 22*al*

Martin Brigdale Page 138*ar*

Peter Cassidy Pages 1, 9, 22*ar*, 88*ar*

Jonathan Gregson Page 37

Richard Jung Pages 44*br*, 71, 126

Mowie Kay Pages 16, 23, 44*ar*, 48, 52, 56, 99,
107, 114, 118, 133, 137

Noelle Kovary Page 142

Adrian Lawrence Pages 29, 34

Jason Lowe Page 110*bl*

Diana Miller Page 110*al*

Steve Painter Pages 2, 22*bl*, 33, 41, 44*bl*,
60*ar*, 76, 88 *al* and *b*, 95, 103, 104, 108,
110*br*, 129, 130, 134,
138*al* and *br*

William Reavell Pages 8*br*, 11, 15,
19, 25, 26, 40, 55, 59, 60*br*, 64, 91, 125, 127,
154

Matt Russell Pages 6, 60*bl*, 65, 72, 75, 78–81,
87, 92, 93, 110*ar*, 138*bl*

Ian Wallace Page 3

Kate Whitaker Pages 27, 30, 32, 35, 58, 113,
117, 135, 150, endpapers

Clare Winfield Pages 4, 5, 8*a* and *bl*, 12, 20,
21, 22*br*, 38, 42, 44*al*, 47, 51, 60*al*, 61, 63, 67,
68, 83, 84, 89, 96, 100, 101, 111, 112, 121,
122, 139, 141, 145–149, 152, 153, 157